REVISE AQA GCSE (9-1)
Religious Studies
CHRISTIANITY AND IS...

REVISION WORKBOOK

AQA

Series Consultant: Harry Smith
Author: Tanya Hill

Also available to support your revision:

Revise GCSE Study Skills Guide   9781447967071

The **Revise GCSE Study Skills Guide** is full of tried-and-trusted hints and tips for how to learn more effectively. It gives you techniques to help you achieve your best — throughout your GCSE studies and beyond!

Revise GCSE Revision Planner   9781447967828

The **Revise GCSE Revision Planner** helps you to plan and organise your time, step-by-step, throughout your GCSE revision. Use this book and wall chart to mastermind your revision.

For the full range of Pearson revision titles across KS2, KS3, GCSE, Functional Skills, AS/A Level and BTEC visit:
www.pearsonschools.co.uk/revise

Pearson

Contents

1 Religious beliefs, teachings and practices

CHRISTIANITY

Key beliefs
- 1 The nature of God I
- 2 Evil and suffering
- 3 The nature of God II
- 4 Creation
- 5 The afterlife

Jesus Christ and salvation
- 6 Jesus as the Son of God
- 7 Crucifixion, resurrection and ascension
- 8 Salvation and atonement

Worship and festivals
- 9 Forms of worship
- 10 Prayer
- 11 Baptism
- 12 Eucharist
- 13 Pilgrimage
- 14 Celebrations

The role of the Church
- 15 The church in the local community
- 16 Sharing faith
- 17 Importance of the worldwide Church I
- 18 Importance of the worldwide Church II

ISLAM

Key beliefs
- 19 The six articles of faith in Sunni Islam
- 20 The five roots of Usul ad-Din in Shi'a Islam
- 21 The Oneness and nature of God
- 22 Angels
- 23 al-Qadr and Akhirah

Authority
- 24 Risalah (prophethood)
- 25 The holy books
- 26 The Imamate in Shi'a Islam

Worship
- 27 The Five Pillars and the Ten Obligatory Acts
- 28 The Shahadah
- 29 Salah I
- 30 Salah II

Duties and festivals
- 31 Sawm
- 32 Zakah and khums
- 33 Hajj
- 34 Jihad
- 35 Festivals and commemorations

2 Thematic studies

Theme A: Relationships and families

Sex, marriage and divorce
- 36 Sexual relationships
- 38 Contraception
- 40 Marriage
- 42 Different relationships
- 44 Divorce and remarriage

Families and gender equality
- 46 Families
- 48 Contemporary issues
- 50 Gender prejudice and discrimination
- 52 Relationships and families: Contrasting beliefs

Theme B: Religion and life

Origins and value of the universe
- 54 Origins of the universe
- 56 The value of the world
- 58 The natural world

Origins and value of human life
- 60 Origins of human life
- 62 Sanctity and quality of life
- 64 Abortion and euthanasia
- 66 Death and the afterlife
- 68 Religion and life: Contrasting beliefs

Theme C: The existence of God and revelation

Philosophical arguments for and against the existence of God
- 70 The existence of God
- 72 Miracles
- 74 Evil and suffering
- 76 Arguments against the existence of God

Nature of the divine and revelation
- 78 Special revelation: Visions
- 80 General revelation
- 82 The existence of God and revelation: Contrasting beliefs

Theme D: Religion, peace and conflict

Religion, violence, terrorism and war
- 84 Peace and justice, forgiveness and reconciliation
- 86 Violence and terrorism
- 88 War and Just War theory
- 90 Holy war
- 92 Pacifism

Religion and belief in 21st-century conflict
- 94 Religion as a cause of conflict
- 96 Religion and peacemaking
- 98 Religion, peace and conflict: Contrasting beliefs

Theme E: Religion, crime and punishment

Religion, crime and the causes of crime
- 100 Good and evil intentions and actions
- 102 Reasons for crime
- 104 Types of crime

Religion and punishment
- 106 Punishment
- 108 The treatment of criminals
- 110 Forgiveness
- 112 The death penalty
- 114 Religion, crime and punishment: Contrasting beliefs

Theme F: Religion, human rights and social justice

Human rights
- 116 Prejudice and discrimination
- 118 Equality and freedom of religious belief
- 120 Social justice

Wealth and poverty
- 122 Responsibilities of wealth
- 124 Exploitation of the poor
- 126 Poverty and charity
- 128 Religion, human rights and social justice: Contrasting beliefs

Theme G: St Mark's Gospel I
- 130 John's preparation for Jesus' ministry
- 131 Jesus' baptism and temptation
- 132 Miracles of Jesus I
- 133 Miracles of Jesus II
- 134 Caesarea Philippi and the transfiguration
- 135 Passion prediction and James and John's request
- 136 The story of Bartimaeus
- 137 The entry into Jerusalem
- 138 The Last Supper
- 139 Jesus in Gethsemane and the trial
- 140 The trial before Pilate, the crucifixion and burial
- 141 The empty tomb

Theme H: St Mark's Gospel II
- 142 The Kingdom of God I
- 143 The Kingdom of God II
- 144 Jesus' relationships: Women
- 145 Jesus' relationships: Gentiles and tax collectors
- 146 Jesus' relationships: The sick
- 147 Faith and discipleship I
- 148 Faith and discipleship II

- 149 Answers

A small bit of small print

AQA publishes Sample Assessment Material and the Specification on its website. This is the official content and this book should be used in conjunction with it. The questions in this Workbook have been written to help you practise every topic in the book. Remember: the real exam questions may not look like this.

Had a go ☐   Nearly there ☐   Nailed it! ☐

Christianity

Key beliefs

Component 1

The nature of God I

1   Which **one** of the following is **not** a characteristic of God used by Christians?

Put a tick (✓) in the box next to the correct answer.

A   Just ☐
B   Omnipotent ☐
C   Loving ☐
D   Inconsistent triad ☑

> This style of question simply requires you to identify the correct answer – it is testing your factual recall. Make sure you read the question carefully. In this example you need to identify which answer is **not** a characteristic used to describe what God is like.

(1 mark)

Guided

2   Give **two** characteristics of God used by Christians to describe God.

1   Christians believe God is just and fair. ....

2   ....

   .... **(2 marks)**

> Complete this answer by giving one more characteristic of God. You don't need to give further information to explain either point.

Guided

3   Give **two** reasons why the presence of evil and suffering challenges the nature of God for Christians.

1   The presence of evil and suffering challenges the nature of God, as if he were omnibenevolent (all-loving), he would want to stop his creation suffering.

> Complete this answer by giving another reason. You don't need to give further information to explain either point.

2   ....

....

.... **(2 marks)**

1

Christianity — Key beliefs — Component 1

Had a go ☐   Nearly there ☐   Nailed it! ☐

Evil and suffering

Guided 1 Explain **two** ways that Christians may respond to evil and suffering in the world.

Christians could be inspired to try to help others who are suffering. They could do this through charity work. For example, Chad Varah established the Samaritans as a result of witnessing the suffering of others while he was working as a priest in London.

> Here, an example from charity work is given, which is supported by further information and an example. Complete this answer by explaining a second way that Christians may respond to evil and suffering. You could use any other example you have studied.

....
....
....
....
....

(4 marks)

2 Explain **two** Christian teachings about why there is evil and suffering in the world.

Refer to sacred writings or another source of Christian belief and teaching in your answer.

> You need to give two different Christian teachings. Make sure you develop each one by adding further explanation or examples. You need to link at least one teaching to a relevant source of scripture that you have studied. You can do this by quoting directly or by summarising in your own words.

....
....
....
....
....
....
....
....
....
....
....
....

(5 marks)

Had a go ☐ Nearly there ☐ Nailed it! ☐

Christianity
Key beliefs
Component 1

The nature of God II

1 'The Trinity helps Christians to understand God.'

Evaluate this statement.

In your answer you should:

- refer to Christian teaching
- give reasoned arguments to support this statement
- give reasoned arguments to support a different point of view
- reach a justified conclusion.

> This type of question requires the skills of analysis and evaluation. You need to consider the statement carefully and think of reasons that may agree and disagree with it. Your reasons must be linked to Christian teachings. After considering all the arguments, you need to give an overall justified conclusion. Remember that there are also 3 marks available for spelling, punctuation and grammar on this question, so check your answer carefully.

....
....
....
....
....
....
....
....
....
....
....
....
....
....
....
....
....
....
....

(12 marks + 3 SPaG marks)

Please complete your answer on your own paper if you need more space.

Christianity
Key beliefs
Component 1

Had a go ☐ Nearly there ☐ Nailed it! ☐

Creation

1 Which **one** of the following is the name of the book in the Bible where the Christian story of creation is found?

Put a tick (✓) in the box next to the correct answer.

- A Genesis ☐
- B Matthew ☐
- C Exodus ☐
- D Mark ☐

> This style of question simply requires you to identify the correct answer. It is testing your factual recall. Make sure you read the question carefully.

(1 mark)

Guided   **2** Explain **two** Christian teachings about the creation of the universe.

Refer to sacred writings or another source of Christian belief and teaching in your answer.

The Bible teaches that the universe was created at a command from God. ....

> This answer starts by giving a Christian teaching from the Bible. You need to develop this by giving further information before going on to explain a second teaching about the creation of the universe that is developed in the same way. Remember to link at least one of your teachings to a relevant source of Christian belief and teaching. You can do this by summarising in your own words or by direct quotation.

(5 marks)

Had a go ☐ Nearly there ☐ Nailed it! ☐

Christianity

Key beliefs

Component 1

The afterlife

1. Give **two** reasons why a belief in the afterlife is important for Christians.

   1 ....
   ....
   ....

   2 ....
   ....
   ....

   > You need to apply your understanding of Christian beliefs about the afterlife to answer this question by giving two reasons why this belief holds great significance for Christians.

   (2 marks)

Guided

2. Explain **two** ways in which a belief in the afterlife will influence Christians today.

   1 A belief in the afterlife will influence Christians to live good lives so that they can be rewarded in heaven and avoid going to hell. ....
   ....
   ....
   ....
   ....
   ....
   ....

   > Two ways that belief in the afterlife affects the lives of Christians today are given in this guided answer. You need to develop each way by giving further information or examples, or by referring to Christian teachings.

   2 A belief in the afterlife will encourage Christians to pray to God more regularly. ....
   ....
   ....
   ....
   ....
   ....
   ....
   ....

   (4 marks)

Christianity

Jesus Christ and salvation

Component 1

Had a go ☐   Nearly there ☐   Nailed it! ☐

Jesus as the Son of God

1 Give **two** Christian beliefs about the incarnation.

   1 ....

   ....

   > The incarnation is the Christian belief that God took human form through Jesus. To answer this question, you need to state two beliefs held by Christians about this idea.

   2 ....

   ....

   (2 marks)

Guided 2 Explain **two** ways in which beliefs about the incarnation influence Christians today.

Christians try to follow the example of Jesus in their lives, as they believe he came to Earth to show them how they should behave. ....

> Two ways in which beliefs about the incarnation affect the lives of Christians today are given in this partial answer. You need to develop each way by giving further information or examples.

....

....

....

....

....

Christians use ideas about the incarnation, which prove that Jesus was the Son of God, to help them understand God better. ....

....

....

....

....

(4 marks)

6

Had a go ☐   Nearly there ☐   Nailed it! ☐

Christianity
Jesus Christ and salvation
Component 1

Crucifixion, resurrection and ascension

Guided 1 'The resurrection of Jesus is more important to Christians than the crucifixion.'

Evaluate this statement.

In your answer you should:

- refer to Christian teaching
- give reasoned arguments to support this statement
- give reasoned arguments to support a different point of view
- reach a justified conclusion.

> Complete this answer by adding further reasons to support each viewpoint and by including some teachings or Bible accounts about the incarnation (for example, the birth, death and resurrection of Jesus). After considering all the arguments, end with an overall justified conclusion. Remember that there are also 3 marks available for spelling, punctuation and grammar for this question, so read through your final answer carefully.

Some Christians may agree with the statement, as the resurrection of Jesus is one of the key beliefs held in Christianity. Jesus came to Earth with the purpose of saving the sins of the whole world and repairing the relationship between God and humanity. The resurrection is evidence that Jesus was the Son of God. ....

....

....

....

....

Some Christians may argue that the crucifixion and resurrection are equally important as without one the other could not have happened.

....

....

....

....

....

....

(12 marks + 3 SPaG marks)

Please complete your answer on your own paper if you need more space.

Christianity — Jesus Christ and salvation — Component 1

Had a go ☐ Nearly there ☐ Nailed it! ☐

Salvation and atonement

1. Which **one** of the following refers to the Christian idea of humans being reconciled and forgiven by God through the death of Jesus?

   Put a tick (✓) in the box next to the correct answer.

   A Salvation ☐
   B Original sin ☐
   C Atonement ☐
   D Sacrifice ☐

   > This style of question simply requires you to identify the correct answer – it is testing your factual recall. Make sure you understand and are able to identify what each word means so you can work out which answer is correct.

   (1 mark)

Guided

2. Explain **two** Christian teachings about salvation.

   Refer to sacred writings or another source of Christian belief and teaching in your answer.

   Christianity teaches that God sent Jesus to Earth as God in human form so that humanity could achieve salvation. ....

   > You could develop this first point by linking it to a teaching from the Bible, such as John 3:16. You then need to add a second teaching and develop it in the same way.

   ....
   ....
   ....
   ....
   ....
   ....
   ....
   ....
   ....
   ....

   (5 marks)

Had a go ☐   Nearly there ☐   Nailed it! ☐

Christianity — Worship and festivals — Component 1

Forms of worship

1 Which **one** of the following is the term used to describe Christian worship that follows a set pattern on a regular basis?

Put a tick (✓) in the box next to the correct answer.

- A Non-liturgical ☐
- B Informal ☐
- C Liturgical ☐
- D Meditation ☐

> Look at the four options carefully. Check your understanding of each term before deciding which one you think correctly answers the question.

(1 mark)

Guided

2 Explain **two** ways in which Christians choose to worship God.

Refer to sacred writings or another source of Christian belief and teaching in your answer.

Some Christians choose to worship God using liturgical worship, which is where Christians worship together following a set pattern and structure.

....
....
....
....
....
....
....
....
....
....
....

> Develop this answer by adding an example or providing further information about liturgical worship (for example, you could mention the Eucharist and give examples of how this is liturgical worship). Then explain a second way that some Christians choose to worship God, such as non-liturgical, private or informal worship. You need to link at least one of your explanations to a quote from the Bible or Book of Common Prayer.

(5 marks)

9

Christianity
Worship and festivals — Component 1

Had a go ☐ Nearly there ☐ Nailed it! ☐

Prayer

Guided 1. Give **two** purposes of prayer for Christians.

1 Christians pray to God to get closer to and communicate with him. ....

2 ....

....

> One purpose of prayer is given. You need to add another purpose of prayer in the second part of this answer. Remember that you are not required to develop these ideas.

(2 marks)

2. Explain **two** contrasting types of Christian prayer.

> Christians have different types of prayer, including set prayers, informal prayers and popular prayers such as the Lord's Prayer. You need to choose two of these types and explain your knowledge about them by giving further information or examples or by referring to Christian teachings.

(4 marks)

Had a go ☐ Nearly there ☐ Nailed it! ☐

Christianity
Worship and festivals
Component 1

Baptism

1 Which **one** of the following is the term used for the outward and visible sign of an invisible and spiritual grace? Does this mean that it works?

   Put a tick (✓) in the box next to the correct answer.

   A Baptism   ☐
   B Sacrament   ☐
   C Community   ☐
   D Font   ☐

   > Look at the four options carefully. Check your understanding of each term before deciding which one you think correctly answers the question.

   (1 mark)

2 Explain **two** contrasting ways in which Christians celebrate the sacrament of baptism.

   > Remember that different Christians practise baptism differently, with some choosing infant baptism whereas others accept only adult baptism. You could also refer to child dedication ceremonies in your answer. You need to develop each way by giving further information or examples or by referring to Christian teachings.

   ....

   (4 marks)

Christianity

Worship and festivals

Component 1

Had a go ☐ Nearly there ☐ Nailed it! ☐

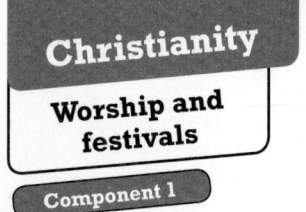

Eucharist

1 'It is more important to pray individually to God than to celebrate the Eucharist.'

Evaluate this statement.

In your answer you should:

- refer to Christian teaching
- give reasoned arguments to support this statement
- give reasoned arguments to support a different point of view
- reach a justified conclusion.

> This type of question requires the skills of analysis and evaluation. You need to consider the statement carefully and think of reasons that may agree and disagree with it, linking your reasons to Christian teachings. After considering all the arguments, end with a justified overall conclusion.

....

(12 marks)

Please complete your answer on your own paper if you need more space.

Had a go ☐ Nearly there ☐ Nailed it! ☐

Christianity
Worship and festivals
Component 1

Pilgrimage

1 'Pilgrimage has no value today.'

Evaluate this statement.

In your answer you should:

- refer to Christian teaching
- give reasoned arguments to support this statement
- give reasoned arguments to support a different point of view
- reach a justified conclusion.

> Consider the statement in the question carefully. It is always good to plan which arguments you will use to agree and disagree before you start writing. For example, here you could consider: other aspects of Christianity that have more importance today; the fact there is no requirement in Christianity to complete a pilgrimage; the personal nature of faith; the importance and meaning of pilgrimage to Christians; the need for Christians to take time out of their busy lives to focus on their faith; the significance of the places they may visit.

....
....
....
....
....
....
....
....
....
....
....
....
....
....
....
....
....
....
.... **(12 marks)**

Please complete your answer on your own paper if you need more space.

Christianity
Worship and festivals — Component 1

Had a go ☐ Nearly there ☐ Nailed it! ☐

Celebrations

1 Give **two** ways in which Christians celebrate Christmas today.

1 ....
....
....

2 ....
....

State two different ways to answer this question successfully. Remember that they should be religious ways rather than just nice things that happen at Christmas.

(2 marks)

Guided

2 Explain **two** ways in which Christians mark the death and resurrection of Jesus at Easter.

Refer to sacred writings or another source of Christian belief and teaching in your answer.

Christians attend special services at Easter to mark the death of Jesus on the cross. There may be a re-enactment of the events of the crucifixion, perhaps with Jesus carrying his cross and being crucified on Good Friday. Christians may think about Jesus' sacrifice and celebrate his resurrection, which reflects key Christian beliefs (as stated in the Bible) in eternal life, God's love for the world in sending Jesus and following Jesus leading to eternal life.

This answer explains how some Christians celebrate Easter by re-enacting key events. It also successfully refers to a teaching from the Bible (from John 3:16), which has been put into the student's own words. Complete the answer by adding a second explanation.

....
....
....
....
....
....
....

(5 marks)

Had a go ☐ Nearly there ☐ Nailed it! ☐

Christianity
The role of the Church
Component 1

The church in the local community

1 'The most important role of the local church is to provide help to those in the community.'

Evaluate this statement.

In your answer you should:

- refer to Christian teaching
- give reasoned arguments to support this statement
- give reasoned arguments to support a different point of view
- reach a justified conclusion.

> Start your answer by offering reasons why Christians may agree with this statement. Next, try to give an alternative point of view. Throughout your answer, make sure you refer to Christian teachings to support the points you make. Remember that not all Christians agree with each other and they may offer differing views for varied reasons. Finally, bring your answer to a close by reaching an overall justified conclusion.

....

(12 marks)

Please complete your answer on your own paper if you need more space.

15

Christianity
The role of the Church
Component 1

Had a go ☐ Nearly there ☐ Nailed it! ☐

Sharing faith

1. Give **two** ways in which Christian churches can help Church growth.

   1 ....

   2 ....

   > You need to give two examples of how individual churches can help the worldwide Church to grow. This could be locally in their own communities, nationally in larger areas or globally across the world.

   (2 marks)

Guided

2. Explain **two** contrasting ways in which the Church supports the growth of Christianity.

   One way the Church supports the growth of Christianity is by organising education classes where those who are not part of the Christian faith can learn more about the Christian religion and engage in debate and discussions about the faith. These courses are known as Alpha courses and they are run in local communities. They encourage people who are not members of the Church community to find out more so they can join the Christian faith. ....

   ....

   > This question requires you to explain how the Church can support the growth of Christianity, so has a similar focus to Question 1, but this time you need to develop your explanation. You can do this by giving further information and specific examples, such as by referring to Christian teachings.

   (4 marks)

Had a go ☐   Nearly there ☐   Nailed it! ☐

Christianity
The role of the Church
Component 1

Importance of the worldwide Church 1

1 'It is the responsibility of every Christian to respond when others are persecuted.'

Evaluate this statement.

In your answer you should:

- refer to Christian teaching
- give reasoned arguments to support this statement
- give reasoned arguments to support a different point of view
- reach a justified conclusion.

> Make sure you offer arguments to support this statement as well as alternative views. You may consider why Christianity teaches that reconciliation is important and give examples of what individual Christians and organisations have done to support this. Remember that some Christians may feel it is difficult for them to help others alone. End your answer with an overall justified conclusion.

(12 marks)

Please complete your answer on your own paper if you need more space.

Christianity

The role of the Church

Component 1

Had a go ☐   Nearly there ☐   Nailed it! ☐

Importance of the worldwide Church II

1 Which **one** of the following is **not** the name of a Christian charity organisation?

Put a tick (✓) in the box next to the correct answer.

   A CAFOD (the Catholic Agency for Overseas Development) ☐
   B Christian Aid ☐
   C Tearfund ☐
   D Muslim Aid ☐

> Read questions like this carefully. Note that here you are asked which answer is **not** the name of a Christian charity.

(1 mark)

Guided

2 Explain **two** ways in which Christian charities work to help those living in poverty.

Refer to sacred writing or another source of Christian belief and teaching in your answer.

An organisation such as CAFOD works to provide food, water and shelter in times of emergency and crisis in the world. ....

....

....

....

> Develop the point here by adding further information, such as by giving a specific example of where CAFOD works and what it has done there or by explaining what its aims are. Then give a second way that Christian charities help those living in poverty. Remember to link either the first or the second way to a source of religious authority such as a teaching from the Bible.

....

....

....

....

....

....

....

....

(5 marks)

Had a go ☐ Nearly there ☐ Nailed it! ☐

Islam
Key beliefs
Component 1

The six articles of faith in Sunni Islam

Guided 1 Give **two** ways that the six articles of faith are expressed by Sunni Muslims.

   1 Muslims recite belief in the Oneness of Allah.
   ....

   2 ....
   ....

> You need to state two different ideas. Note that the question is not asking you to state what the six articles of faith are, but how they are expressed or used by Sunni Muslims.

(2 marks)

Guided 2 'The six articles of faith are the same as the five roots of Usul ad-Din.'

Evaluate this statement.

In your answer you should:

- refer to Muslim teaching
- give reasoned arguments to support this statement
- give reasoned arguments to support a different point of view
- reach a justified conclusion.

> Sunni Muslims have the six articles of faith and Shi'a Muslims have the five roots of Usul ad-Din. Consider in your answer the beliefs within them that are the same and those that are different. Conclude your answer with an overall justified summary, then read it through carefully to check for spelling, punctuation and grammar.

It is possible to see similarities between the six articles of faith and the five roots of Usul ad-Din, so some may argue that the basis of them is the same. ....

....

....

....

....

....

....

....

....

....

....

(12 marks + 3 SPaG marks)

Please complete your answer on your own paper if you need more space.

Islam
Key beliefs — Component 1

Had a go ☐   Nearly there ☐   Nailed it! ☐

The five roots of Usul ad-Din in Shi'a Islam

Guided 1. Give **two** beliefs contained in the five roots of Usul ad-Din for Shi'a Muslims.

1. One of the five roots is Tawhid (the Oneness of Allah). ....

2. ....

....

This question requires you to give two different ideas. Remember that there are five roots to choose from.

(2 marks)

Guided 2. Explain **two** ways the five roots of Usul ad-Din are seen in the lives of Shi'a Muslims today.

One of the five roots is about the Day of Judgement, so Shi'a Muslims may live with the awareness that Allah will judge them after death. This may mean that they try to live according to the rules set down by Allah, for example by following the Five Pillars of Islam.

In this answer, one way is given that is then supported with further detail and an example. To complete this answer, choose a different way and explain fully how it may cause a Shi'a Muslim to behave.

....

....

....

....

....

....

....

....

....

(4 marks)

Had a go ☐ Nearly there ☐ Nailed it! ☐

Islam — Key beliefs — Component 1

The Oneness and nature of God

Guided 1 'The best way of understanding God is through Tawhid.'

Evaluate this statement.

In your answer you should:

- refer to Muslim teaching
- give reasoned arguments to support this statement
- give reasoned arguments to support a different point of view
- reach a justified conclusion.

> Begin your answer by offering arguments that agree with the statement. Then develop your answer by adding arguments that offer a different view; some ideas are given in the partial answer here. Be sure to refer to Muslim teachings where appropriate. End your answer by considering all your arguments and giving a justified conclusion – this could be your opinion. There are also 3 marks available for spelling, punctuation and grammar for this question, so read your final answer through carefully.

....
....
....
....
....
....

Although Muslims view Tawhid as central to understanding Allah, other terms and methods can be used. For example, Muslims believe Allah is transcendent, meaning he is beyond human understanding, as well as immanent (close and acting within the world). This demonstrates Allah's powerful nature, yet is a little contradictory for some people as he is seen as being both beyond human understanding but also close to and acting within the world.

....
....
....
....
....
....

(12 marks + 3 SPaG marks)

Please complete your answer on your own paper if you need more space.

Islam

Key beliefs — Component 1

Had a go ☐   Nearly there ☐   Nailed it! ☐

Angels

1. Which **one** of the following is the name of the angel who dictated the Qur'an to Muhammad?

   Put a tick (✓) in the box next to the correct answer.

   A   Jibril   ☐
   B   Mika'il   ☐
   C   Izra'il   ☐
   D   Allah   ☐

   > Read all the possible answers carefully. Make sure you decide which one is correct.

   (1 mark)

Guided

2. Explain **two** Muslim teachings about the importance of angels in Islam.

   Refer to sacred writings or another source of Muslim belief and teaching in your answer.

   Angels are important in Islam as they are messengers between Allah and humans. For example, Muhammad received the Qur'an from the angel Jibril and, without this important message, Muslims today would not have the guidance of the words of Allah. The Qur'an teaches that Jibril appeared to Muhammad over 23 years and taught him the words of the Qur'an.

   > Remember that angels have different and important roles in Islam. For example, the Angel of Death reminds Muslims to follow Allah's guidance, whereas another angel reminds Muslims of the rewards that await them in heaven. You could include these in your answer. To complete this answer, choose a second teaching and then develop your explanation by adding an example or further information. The guided answer links to the Qur'an, so the requirement to refer to sacred writings has been met, but you could practise linking to a source of Muslim religious authority in your answer.

   ....
   ....
   ....
   ....
   ....
   ....
   ....
   ....
   ....

   (5 marks)

Had a go ☐   Nearly there ☐   Nailed it! ☐

Islam

Key beliefs

Component 1

al-Qadr and Akhirah

1 'Muslims should be scared of the Day of Judgement.'

Evaluate this statement.

In your answer you should:

- refer to Muslim teaching
- give reasoned arguments to support this statement
- give reasoned arguments to support a different point of view
- reach a justified conclusion.

> You need to include arguments that agree with the statement, as well as alternative views. For example, you could mention: descriptions in the Qur'an of hell as a place of pain and torment; Muslims' knowledge that they will be judged after death; life as a test of how Muslims use their free will; Allah as merciful; teachings that suggest Muslims should enjoy the life Allah has given to them. Remember to refer to Muslim teachings throughout your answer and to end with a justified conclusion before checking your answer for spelling, punctuation and grammar.

....
....
....
....
....
....
....
....
....
....
....
....
....
....
....
....
....
....
....
....

(12 marks + 3 SPaG marks)

Please complete your answer on your own paper if you need more space.

Islam — Authority — Component 1

Risalah (prophethood)

1. Which **one** of the following is the name of the prophet in Islam who had his faith tested by Allah by being asked to sacrifice his son?

    Put a tick (✓) in the box next to the correct answer.

    A Muhammad ☐
    B Isma'il ☐
    C Ibrahim ☐
    D Jibril ☐

    > Read all the possible answers carefully. Make sure you can identify who each person is before deciding which answer is correct.

    (1 mark)

2. Explain **two** Muslim teachings about Risalah (prophethood).

    Refer to sacred writings or another source of Muslim belief and teaching in your answer.

    > This question requires you to identify two different teachings and then develop each one by giving a full explanation. You also need to link at least one teaching to a source of Islamic religious authority, such as the Qur'an, by either quoting directly or summarising in your own words.

    ....

    (5 marks)

Had a go ☐ Nearly there ☐ Nailed it! ☐

Islam

Authority

Component 1

The holy books

Guided

1 Give **two** ways that Muslims use the Qur'an in their lives.

1 Muslims read passages from the Qur'an in the Jummah service in the mosque. ....

2 ....

....

> One idea is given; you simply need to state a second, different idea. You don't need to explain them.

(2 marks)

2 Explain **two** ways that beliefs about the Qur'an impact on the lives of Muslims.

....

....

....

....

....

....

....

....

....

....

....

....

....

....

> Muslims accept the Qur'an as the complete, unaltered words of Allah, so it is central to their faith. When answering this question, consider the effect the Qur'an may have on Muslims – how might they turn to it or use it in their lives? You need to identify two different impacts and then develop each one fully.

(4 marks)

Islam — Authority — Component 1

Had a go ☐ Nearly there ☐ Nailed it! ☐

The Imamate in Shi'a Islam

1 'The imam is very important in Shi'a Islam as a source of authority.'

Evaluate this statement.

In your answer you should:

- refer to Muslim teaching
- give reasoned arguments to support this statement
- give reasoned arguments to support a different point of view
- reach a justified conclusion.

> Sunni and Shi'a Muslims have different understandings of the role of the imam. For Sunni Muslims, the imam simply leads prayers in the mosque, whereas Shi'a Muslims view imams as divinely appointed by Allah. Consider these ideas when thinking about arguments to support the statement, as well as those that offer a different view. Remember to refer to Muslim teaching throughout your answer. End with a justified conclusion based on the arguments you have included before checking your answer for spelling, punctuation and grammar.

....
....
....
....
....
....
....
....
....
....
....
....
....
....
....
....
....
....
....
....

(12 marks + 3 SPaG marks)

Please complete your answer on your own paper if you need more space.

Had a go ☐   Nearly there ☐   Nailed it! ☐

Islam

Worship

Component 1

The Five Pillars and the Ten Obligatory Acts

> Guided

1 'The Five Pillars of Islam are the basis of the religion.'

Evaluate this statement.

In your answer you should:

- refer to Muslim teaching
- give reasoned arguments to support this statement
- give reasoned arguments to support a different point of view
- reach a justified conclusion.

> Start by giving reasons to agree with the statement. Next, consider alternative views and what reasons may be given for them. Remember that Shi'a Muslims recognise the Five Pillars but incorporate them into the Ten Obligatory Acts. Refer to Muslim teachings throughout before ending with a justified conclusion.

Some Muslims may agree with the statement, as the Five Pillars of Islam are the basic duties that all Muslims have to perform. ....

....

....

....

....

....

....

The Ten Obligatory Acts are more important to Shi'a Muslims (although four of the Five Pillars of Islam are included in the Ten Obligatory Acts); therefore they would be likely to support a different view. ....

....

....

....

....

....

....

....

....

(12 marks)

Please complete your answer on your own paper if you need more space.

Islam — Worship — Component 1

Had a go ☐ *Nearly there* ☐ *Nailed it!* ☐

The Shahadah

Guided

1 Give **two** occasions when Muslims say the Shahadah.

1 Muslims whisper the words of the Shahadah into the ears of newborn babies. ....

2 ....
....

> The Shahadah is the declaration of faith, which includes belief in one God (Allah) and Muhammad as the Prophet of Allah. Complete this guided answer by giving a second occasion when the Shahadah may be spoken.

(2 marks)

2 Explain **two** contrasting understandings of the Shahadah.

> Remember that Sunni and Shi'a Muslims recognise the Shahadah slightly differently. You can show this in your answer to this question. Remember to develop fully each point you make by supporting it with further detail and examples, and by referring to Muslim teachings.

(4 marks)

Had a go ☐   Nearly there ☐   Nailed it! ☐

Islam

Worship

Component 1

Salah I

1. Which **one** of the following is the term used to describe the weekly Salah that takes place on a Friday after midday in the mosque?

   Put a tick (✓) in the box next to the correct answer.

   A Rak'ahs ☐
   B Wudu ☐
   C Ka'aba ☐
   D Jummah ☐

   > Check your understanding of each term before deciding which one best answers the question.

   (1 mark)

2. Give **two** reasons why Salah is important in Islam.

   1 ....
   ....
   ....

   > Make sure you state two different reasons. You don't need to **develop** them.

   2 ....
   ....

   (2 marks)

Guided

3. Explain **two** Muslim teachings about how Salah should be performed in Islam.

   Refer to sacred writings or another source of Muslim belief and teaching in your answer.

   Muslims are expected through Salah to worship Allah and recognise his power. For example, Islam teaches that prayer verses should be read from the Qur'an when Salah is performed. ....

   > Give two reasons and then develop each one by adding further information or detail. You also need to link at least one of your reasons to a teaching from a source of Islamic religious authority, such as the Qur'an.

   ....
   ....
   ....
   ....
   ....
   ....
   ....
   ....
   ....

   (5 marks)

29

Islam: Worship — Component 1

Salah II

Had a go ☐   Nearly there ☐   Nailed it! ☐

1 'Muslims should not have to pray five times a day; they should be able to pray when they want.'

Evaluate this statement.

In your answer you should:

- refer to Muslim teaching
- give reasoned arguments to support this statement
- give reasoned arguments to support a different point of view
- reach a justified conclusion.

> Remember that Muslims may hold different beliefs about this statement. For example, Sunni and Shi'a Muslims have different understandings of Salah. Make sure you include arguments to both support and disagree with the statement, and refer to Muslim teachings throughout. End with a justified conclusion based on the arguments you have developed in your answer.

(12 marks)

Please complete your answer on your own paper if you need more space.

Had a go ☐   Nearly there ☐   Nailed it! ☐

Islam
Duties and festivals
Component 1

Sawm

Guided 1 'There is no benefit to fasting today.'

Evaluate this statement.

In your answer you should:

- refer to Muslim teaching
- give reasoned arguments to support this statement
- give reasoned arguments to support a different point of view
- reach a justified conclusion.

> Many Muslims accept Sawm (fasting) as a duty given to them by Allah. This answer starts by showing an awareness of why this Pillar is so important to Muslims in terms of the benefits it brings them.

Some Muslims may agree with the statement. They may argue that the supposed benefits of fasting (for example, getting closer to Allah) could be achieved through other means. For example, ...
....
....
....
....
....

Many Muslims would disagree with the statement because they believe Sawm is a duty from Allah and it is one of the Five Pillars of Islam. Many Muslims believe there are many benefits to Sawm, such as ....
....
....
....
....
....

Having considered all these views, overall I conclude ....
....
....
....
....
....

(12 marks)

Please complete your answer on your own paper if you need more space.

31

Islam
Duties and festivals
Component 1

Had a go ☐ Nearly there ☐ Nailed it! ☐

Zakah and khums

1 Which **one** of the following is the name given to describe the compulsory tax given by Shi'a Muslims of 20 per cent of surplus income?

Put a tick (✓) in the box next to the correct answer.

- **A** Zakah ☐
- **B** Salah ☐
- **C** Khums ☐
- **D** Sunni ☐

> Make sure you know what each term means. Remember that there are key differences between Sunni and Shi'a Muslims that you need to be aware of.

(1 mark)

Guided **2** Explain **two** Muslim teachings about Zakah.

Refer to sacred writings or another source of Muslim belief and teaching in your answer.

Muslims believe Zakah is a duty as it is one of the Five Pillars of Islam. ....

....

....

....

....

....

> This type of question asks you to give two reasons and then develop each one by giving further information or detail. You need to link at least one of your reasons to a teaching from a source of Islamic religious authority, such as the Qur'an, by either quoting directly or summarising in your own words.

Muslims also believe Zakah should be used to help the poor and needy. This is a responsibility for every Muslim, as explained in the Qur'an.

....

....

....

....

....

(5 marks)

32

Had a go ☐   Nearly there ☐   Nailed it! ☐

Islam
Duties and festivals
Component 1

Hajj

1 'Money used to complete Hajj could be better spent.'

Evaluate this statement.

In your answer you should:

- refer to Muslim teaching
- give reasoned arguments to support this statement
- give reasoned arguments to support a different point of view
- reach a justified conclusion.

> Start by considering why some people (for example, some Muslims and some non-religious believers) may agree with this statement. Then develop your answer by giving arguments to support other perspectives. Link your reasons to Muslim teachings throughout. After considering all the arguments, end with a justified conclusion.

....

(12 marks)

Please complete your answer on your own paper if you need more space.

Islam

Duties and festivals

Component 1

Had a go ☐ Nearly there ☐ Nailed it! ☐

Jihad

Guided 1 Give **two** examples of rules applied for lesser jihad.

1 Lesser jihad should be fought only as a last resort.
....

2 ....

....

> Complete this answer by giving a second, different idea. You simply need to state your answer. You don't need to explain it.

(2 marks)

2 Explain **two** contrasting understandings of jihad.

....

....

> Identify two ways that Muslims understand jihad. Develop each way fully by supporting it with further detail and an example.

....
....
....
....
....
....
....
....
....
....
....
....

(4 marks)

Had a go ☐ Nearly there ☐ Nailed it! ☐

Islam
Duties and festivals
Component 1

Festivals and commemorations

1 Which **one** of the following is a festival celebrated on the tenth day of Muharran?

   Put a tick (✓) in the box next to the correct answer.

   A Ashura ☐
   B Id-ul-Fitr ☐
   C Salah ☐
   D Zakah ☐

   > Identify which answer is correct from the options given. Make sure you understand what each word means.

   (1 mark)

2 'Celebrating festivals is an important part of belonging to Islam.'

   Evaluate this statement.

   In your answer you should:

   - refer to Muslim teaching
   - give reasoned arguments to support this statement
   - give reasoned arguments to support a different point of view
   - reach a justified conclusion.

   > This type of question requires the skills of analysis and evaluation. Consider the statement carefully and then identify reasons that support it as well as those that offer a different view. Link all your reasons to Muslim teachings before ending with an overall justified conclusion.

   ....
   ....
   ....
   ....
   ....
   ....
   ....
   ....
   ....
   ....
   ....
   ....
   ....

   (12 marks)

   Please complete your answer on your own paper if you need more space.

Christianity — Theme A — Components 2A and 2B

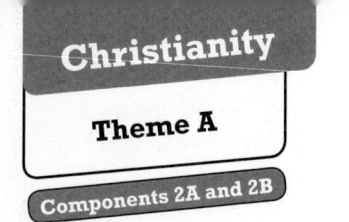

Had a go ☐ Nearly there ☐ Nailed it! ☐

Sexual relationships

1 'The only place for a sexual relationship is within marriage.'

Evaluate this statement.

In your answer you:

- should give reasoned arguments in support of this statement
- should give reasoned arguments to support a different point of view
- should refer to religious arguments
- may refer to non-religious arguments
- should reach a justified conclusion.

> This type of question asks you to evaluate the given statement. Make sure you provide arguments that agree with the statement – these could be from a Christian or a Muslim perspective – as well as alternative views, which may include non-religious arguments. End your answer with a considered overall conclusion. You can use the bulleted points as a checklist to ensure you cover all elements of the question. Finally, read through your answer carefully to check for spelling, punctuation and grammar, as there are 3 marks available for this.

....

(12 marks + 3 SPaG marks)

Please complete your answer on your own paper if you need more space.

Had a go ☐   Nearly there ☐   Nailed it! ☐

Islam — Theme A — Components 2A and 2B

Sexual relationships

1 Which **one** of the following is a term used to describe a person who is in a sexual relationship with a person of the same gender?

Put a tick (✓) in the box next to the correct answer.

A Heterosexual ☐
B Homosexual ☐
C Celibate ☐
D Chaste ☐

> Look at the four options carefully. It is good revision practice to check your understanding of each term before deciding which one you think correctly answers the question.

(1 mark)

Guided

2 Explain **two** religious beliefs about relationships.

Refer to sacred writings or another source of religious belief and teaching in your answer.

Islam has strict views on relationships, believing that only heterosexual relationships (between a man and a woman) are allowed.

....

> This question asks you to explain two religious beliefs about relationships generally. You could include beliefs about heterosexuality or homosexuality, or ideas about marriage. You could answer from a Muslim or a Christian perspective, or refer to both religions. This guided answer gives two Muslim beliefs for you to develop further. Remember to link at least one belief to a source of religious teaching, such as the Qur'an.

....
....
....
....
....

Muslims believe sexual relationships before marriage are wrong. ....

....
....
....
....
....
....
....

(5 marks)

Christianity

Theme A — Components 2A and 2B

Had a go ☐ Nearly there ☐ Nailed it! ☐

Contraception

1 Which **one** of the following is the term used to refer to making a decision about when to have a family and how big a family will be?

Put a tick (✓) in the box next to the correct answer.

  A Family planning ☐
  B Procreation ☐
  C Contraception ☐
  D Polygamy ☐

> Look at the four options carefully. It is good revision practice to check your understanding of each term before deciding which one you think correctly answers the question.

(1 mark)

Guided

2 Give **two** religious beliefs about the use of contraception being wrong.

1 Many Christians believe the use of contraception is wrong, as they believe God intends sexual relationships to be for procreation (having children). ....

2 ....

....

....

> This type of question simply asks you to state two different religious beliefs – you don't need to explain them. The first belief here is Christian; you need to add a second, different religious belief, which could be from Christianity or Islam.

(2 marks)

3 Give **two** reasons why a religious couple may accept the use of contraception.

1 ....

....

....

....

2 ....

....

....

> Make sure you state two different reasons. You don't need to develop them. You could answer from a Muslim or a Christian perspective, or refer to both religions.

(2 marks)

Had a go ☐   Nearly there ☐   Nailed it! ☐

Islam

Theme A

Components 2A and 2B

Contraception

1 'The use of contraception is against religion.'

Evaluate this statement.

In your answer you:

- should give reasoned arguments in support of this statement
- should give reasoned arguments to support a different point of view
- should refer to religious arguments
- may refer to non-religious arguments
- should reach a justified conclusion.

> Use the bullet points to the left as a checklist to help you answer this question. You can refer to both Muslim and Christian beliefs in your answer, as well as non-religious views. Remember to support the religious arguments with reference to sources of religious belief and teaching. End with a justified conclusion based on the arguments you have given, before reading your answer back carefully to check for spelling, punctuation and grammar.

(12 marks + 3 SPaG marks)

Please complete your answer on your own paper if you need more space.

Christianity — Theme A
Components 2A and 2B

Had a go ☐ Nearly there ☐ Nailed it! ☐

Marriage

Guided 1 'Marriage should be for life.'

Evaluate this statement.

In your answer you:

- should give reasoned arguments in support of this statement
- should give reasoned arguments to support a different point of view
- should refer to religious arguments
- may refer to non-religious arguments
- should reach a justified conclusion.

> This question focuses on the nature of marriage, but you may also want to revise the topic of divorce to help answer this question. Make sure you provide arguments that agree with the statement – these could be from a Christian or a Muslim perspective – as well as alternative views that may include non-religious arguments. End with a considered, overall conclusion. Finally, check your answer carefully for spelling, punctuation and grammar.

Many Christians agree with the statement, believing that marriage is intended for life, as the vows made before God during the marriage ceremony are when a couple promises to be together until death.

....

....

....

....

....

....

....

....

....

....

....

....

....

....

....

....

....

....

(12 marks + 3 SPaG marks)

Please complete your answer on your own paper if you need more space.

Had a go ☐ Nearly there ☐ Nailed it! ☐

Islam — Theme A — Components 2A and 2B

Marriage

Guided 1. Give **two** religious beliefs about the nature of marriage.

1. Muslims believe Allah intends for a married couple to have children. ....

2. ....

....

> The focus of this question is the 'nature of marriage' – this means what marriage is intended to be like. Remember that Muslims and Christians have strict views on this. One religious belief is stated – you need to add a second.

(2 marks)

Guided 2. Explain **two** religious beliefs about the purpose of marriage.

Refer to sacred writings or another source of religious belief and teaching in your answer.

Islam teaches that Allah created man and woman for each other, so most Muslims believe the main purpose of marriage is to bring a man and a woman together in order to have children and start a family. ....

....

....

....

> This answer gives two Muslim beliefs – remember that you can answer from a Muslim or a Christian perspective, or refer to both religions in your answer. Develop each belief by adding further information or examples. Make sure that you link at least one to a source of religious authority, such as the Qur'an.

Islam also teaches that Allah intends marriage to allow for the sharing of love, companionship and sex between a man and a woman in a committed relationship. ....

....

....

....

....

....

....

....

(5 marks)

Christianity

Theme A — Components 2A and 2B

Had a go ☐ Nearly there ☐ Nailed it! ☐

Different relationships

1 Give **two** religious beliefs about cohabitation.

1 ....
....
....
....

2 ....
....
....

> Remember that cohabitation is when a couple live together without being married. You need to state two different religious beliefs about this idea, which could be from a Christian or a Muslim perspective.

(2 marks)

Guided   **2** Explain **two** contrasting beliefs in contemporary British society about homosexual relationships.

In your answer you should refer to the main religious tradition of Great Britain and one or more other religious traditions.

Traditional Islamic teachings forbid homosexual relationships and do not recognise same-sex marriage.
....
....
....
....
....
....

> This style of question asks you to give two contrasting religious beliefs – one must be from Christianity (the main religious tradition of Great Britain) and the second could be from Christianity or Islam. This answer starts each belief; you need to complete each one by developing the points. You could do this by giving further information or examples, or by referring to religious teachings.

A contrasting belief can be seen in Christianity, as some modern Christians challenge traditional Christian attitudes against homosexual relationships. ....
....
....
....
....
....
....
....

(4 marks)

42

Had a go ☐   Nearly there ☐   Nailed it! ☐

Islam — Theme A — Components 2A and 2B

Different relationships

Guided

1 'Same-sex marriages should not be supported by religious believers.'

Evaluate this statement.

In your answer you:

- should give reasoned arguments in support of this statement
- should give reasoned arguments to support a different point of view
- should refer to religious arguments
- may refer to non-religious arguments
- should reach a justified conclusion.

> Some religious believers may agree with this statement and some may have alternative views. Think about the different reasons that may be offered to support each viewpoint, with reference to religious teachings and non-religious arguments. End with a justified conclusion before checking your answer for spelling, punctuation and grammar.

Most Muslims would agree with the statement as Islam traditionally forbids same-sex relationships. Islam teaches that Allah intends marriage to be between one man and one woman, to allow for procreation.

....

(12 marks + 3 SPaG marks)

Please complete your answer on your own paper if you need more space.

Christianity — Theme A — Components 2A and 2B

Had a go ☐ Nearly there ☐ Nailed it! ☐

Divorce and remarriage

1 Give **two** religious beliefs about divorce.

   1 ....
   ....
   ....

   2 ....
   ....
   ....

   > Remember that some religious believers accept divorce, whereas others don't; you could include both in your answer. This question simply asks you to state two beliefs – you don't need to develop them.

   (2 marks)

Guided

2 Explain **two** religious beliefs about remarriage.

   Refer to sacred writings or another source of religious belief and teaching in your answer.

   Catholic Christians do not accept remarriage because they do not recognise or allow divorce. ....
   ....
   ....
   ....
   ....
   ....

   > The first part of this answer gives a Christian (Catholic) belief, while the second part is from a Protestant Christian perspective. Develop each part of the answer by giving more information or further explanation. You are also required to link one of the beliefs you present to a source of religious authority, such as the Bible.

   Many Protestant Christians accept remarriage as they recognise that sometimes marriages do not work out. They may argue that marriage remains the best environment to provide stability for the family unit and so would support a divorced person getting married again to someone else. ....
   ....
   ....
   ....
   ....

   (5 marks)

Had a go ☐   Nearly there ☐   Nailed it! ☐

Islam — Theme A — Components 2A and 2B

Divorce and remarriage

1. Which **one** of the following means the legal ending of a marriage?

   Put a tick (✓) in the box next to the correct answer.

   A Remarriage ☐
   B Divorce ☐
   C Monogamy ☐
   D Polygamy ☐

   This question is testing your factual recall. Check your understanding of each term carefully before deciding which one you think is correct.

   (1 mark)

> Guided

2. Give **two** religious beliefs about divorce.

   1 Many Muslims believe divorce is acceptable only as a last resort. ....

   2 ....

   This style of question simply asks for two different ideas to be stated – you don't need to develop the points you make. One religious belief about divorce is given in this guided answer. You can add another point from just one religious tradition or from both Christianity and Islam.

   (2 marks)

3. Give **two** religious beliefs about remarriage.

   1 ....

   2 ....

   Christians hold differing views about remarriage. For example, Catholics don't recognise divorce and so see no need for remarriage, yet many Protestants accept remarriage. In contrast, in Islam divorcees are actively encouraged to remarry. You can include any relevant religious beliefs to answer this question successfully.

   (2 marks)

45

Christianity

Theme A

Components 2A and 2B

Had a go ☐   Nearly there ☐   Nailed it! ☐

Families

Guided

1 'A nuclear family provides the best environment in which to raise children.'

Evaluate this statement.

In your answer you:

- should give reasoned arguments in support of this statement
- should give reasoned arguments to support a different point of view
- should refer to religious arguments
- may refer to non-religious arguments
- should reach a justified conclusion.

> Remember that there are different types of family: nuclear, extended, blended, single-parent and same-sex. Provide arguments to agree with the statement, as well as alternative views. Include Christian and Muslim perspectives (supported by references to religious sources), as well as non-religious views. For example, you might consider why some Muslims argue that an extended family is just as valuable as a nuclear family. End with a developed conclusion before reading through your answer to check for spelling, punctuation and grammar.

Christians believe the family is important and may consider a nuclear family to be the ideal family unit, where children can be raised in a positive, stable and nurturing environment. They may feel that the nuclear family closely reflects the idea of family in the Bible.

....

....

....

....

....

....

....

....

....

....

....

....

....

....

....

(12 marks + 3 SPaG marks)

Please complete your answer on your own paper if you need more space.

Had a go ☐   Nearly there ☐   Nailed it! ☐

Islam — Theme A — Components 2A and 2B

Families

1 Give **two** religious beliefs about the purpose of family.

   1 ....

   2 ....

> This style of question simply asks you to state two different religious beliefs – you don't need to develop the points you make. You can answer from just one religious tradition or from both Christianity and Islam.

(2 marks)

Guided

2 Explain **two** religious beliefs about the nature of family.

Refer to sacred writings or another source of religious belief and teaching in your answer.

Many quotes in the Qur'an talk about family and teach young people to have respect for their elders. Muslims traditionally support extended families, where many generations live together and support each other, so that elderly members can be cared for. ....

> The focus of this question is what religious believers think a family should be like. Remember that, in Islam, many Muslims support the idea of an extended family, whereas in Great Britain it is more traditional to find a nuclear family. One belief from Islam is given here, which you need to develop further. You should also add a second belief, which could be from Islam or Christianity. Remember to link your answer to a source of religious belief and teaching.

(5 marks)

Christianity

Theme A

Components 2A and 2B

Had a go ☐   Nearly there ☐   Nailed it! ☐

Contemporary issues

1. Which **one** of the following is the term used to describe the idea of both genders having equal status?

   Put a tick (✓) in the box next to the correct answer.

   A Cohabitation ☐
   B Gender prejudice ☐
   C Gender discrimination ☐
   D Gender equality ☐

   The possible answers are similar, so look at them carefully. Check your understanding of each term before deciding which one you think is correct.

   (1 mark)

2. Explain **two** religious beliefs about the role of women in the family.

   Refer to sacred writings or another source of religious belief and teaching in your answer.

   This question asks about the role of women in the family, but in your answer you may need to talk about the contrasting roles of women and men. Remember that you can include traditional religious views, as well as more modern perspectives. This style of question also asks you to refer to a source of religious authority, such as the Bible, by either quoting directly or summarising in your own words.

   ....
   ....
   ....
   ....
   ....
   ....
   ....
   ....
   ....
   ....
   ....
   ....
   ....
   ....
   ....

   (5 marks)

48

Had a go ☐ Nearly there ☐ Nailed it! ☐

Islam

Theme A

Components 2A and 2B

Contemporary issues

1 Give **two** religious beliefs about polygamy.

   1 ....
   ....
   ....
   2 ....
   ....
   ....

> This style of question simply asks for two different beliefs to be stated – you don't need to develop the points you make. You can answer from just one religious tradition or from both Christianity and Islam. For the topic of polygamy, it is important to recognise that it is supported in Islam but not in Christianity.

(2 marks)

Guided

2 Explain **two** religious beliefs about same-sex parents.

Refer to sacred writings or another source of religious belief and teaching in your answer.

Muslims traditionally do not support same-sex parents, believing that the family should include a mother and a father. They look to traditional Islamic teachings that support this view. ....

> One belief from Islam is outlined here. You need to complete this explanation by giving examples from relevant Islamic teachings. Then add and develop a second belief, which could be from Islam or Christianity.

....
....
....
....
....
....
....
....
....

(5 marks)

49

Christianity — Theme A (Components 2A and 2B)

Had a go ☐   Nearly there ☐   Nailed it! ☐

Gender prejudice and discrimination

1 'There should be equality between men and women in religion.'

Evaluate this statement.

In your answer you:

- should give reasoned arguments in support of this statement
- should give reasoned arguments to support a different point of view
- should refer to religious arguments
- may refer to non-religious arguments
- should reach a justified conclusion.

> This type of question asks you to evaluate the given statement. You will need to provide arguments to agree with the statement, as well as alternative views. You may want to include Christian and Muslim perspectives (supported by references to religious sources), as well as non-religious views. End with a well-developed conclusion before reading through your writing carefully to check for spelling, punctuation and grammar.

(12 marks + 3 SPaG marks)

Please complete your answer on your own paper if you need more space.

Had a go ☐ Nearly there ☐ Nailed it! ☐

Islam

Theme A

Components 2A and 2B

Gender prejudice and discrimination

1. Which **one** of the following means the belief that one gender is better than another?

   Put a tick (✓) in the box next to the correct answer.

   A Gender discrimination ☐
   B Gender equality ☐
   C Genderisation ☐
   D Gender prejudice ☐

   > The possible answers are similar, so check your understanding of each term carefully before deciding which one is correct. Remember that prejudice is an opinion while discrimination is an action.

   (1 mark)

> **Guided**

2. Explain **two** religious beliefs about gender discrimination being wrong.

   Refer to sacred writings or another source of religious belief and teaching in your answer.

   Many Christians today believe God created all humans to be equal. ....

   ....

   ....

   > This type of question asks you to give two different religious beliefs and explain them fully. You also need to link one of the beliefs you present to a source of religious authority, such as the Qur'an. Complete this answer by developing each belief and linking one of them to a relevant source of religious belief and teaching.

   ....

   ....

   ....

   ....

   ....

   Many Muslims believe gender discrimination is wrong as Islam teaches that Allah treats men and women equally and judges them in the same way after death. ....

   ....

   ....

   ....

   ....

   ....

   (5 marks)

Christianity Islam

Theme A

Components 2A and 2B

Had a go ☐ Nearly there ☐ Nailed it! ☐

Relationships and families: Contrasting beliefs

Guided

1 Explain **two** similar religious beliefs about the use of contraception.

In your answer you must refer to one or more religious traditions.

Catholics believe artificial methods of contraception, such as the Pill and condoms, are wrong as they prevent the main purpose of sex, which Catholic teachings state is to have children (procreation).

....

....

....

....

> This style of question asks you to consider two similar beliefs within a religious tradition (for example, within Christianity) or across two different religious traditions (such as Christianity and Islam). This answer gives two similar beliefs and a reason for each. Develop each belief by adding further explanation or examples.

Some Muslims view artificial methods of contraception as wrong, but believe natural forms of contraception can be allowed as they allow for the possibility of a child to be conceived if Allah wishes. ....

....

....

....

(4 marks)

2 Explain **two** contrasting beliefs in contemporary British society about a couple considering a sexual relationship before marriage.

In your answer you should refer to the main religious tradition of Great Britain and one or more other religious traditions.

....

....

....

....

....

....

....

....

> This style of question asks you to consider two contrasting religious beliefs – one must be from the main religious tradition of Great Britain (Christianity), the second belief could be from Christianity or Islam. Take care to check that your second belief is different to (contrasts with) the first.

(4 marks)

Had a go ☐   Nearly there ☐   Nailed it! ☐

Christianity / Islam
Theme A
Components 2A and 2B

Relationships and families: Contrasting beliefs

1. Explain **two** similar religious beliefs about the importance of saving sexual relationships for after marriage.

   In your answer you must refer to one or more religious traditions.

   ....
   ....
   ....
   ....
   ....
   ....
   ....
   ....
   ....
   ....

   > When answering this question, make sure you offer two similar (rather than different) beliefs. Both Christians and Muslims hold traditional views about sexual relationships being a gift from God and procreation being the main purpose of sex. You could include these views within your answer.

   (4 marks)

Guided

2. Explain **two** contrasting beliefs in contemporary British society about same-sex marriage.

   In your answer you should refer to the main religious tradition of Great Britain and one or more other religious traditions.

   Traditional Islamic teachings forbid homosexual relationships and do not recognise same-sex marriage.
   ....
   ....
   ....
   ....

   In contrast, some modern Christians have challenged traditional Christian attitudes against homosexual relationships. ....
   ....
   ....
   ....
   ....

   > Two beliefs that contrast each other (are not the same) are outlined here. You can give one belief from Christianity and one from Islam, or two different beliefs from the same religion. Complete the answer by explaining each belief fully.

   (4 marks)

Christianity

Theme B — Components 2A and 2B

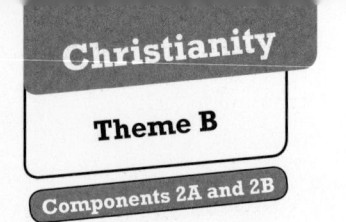

Had a go ☐   Nearly there ☐   Nailed it! ☐

Origins of the universe

1. 'Religious accounts of the origins of the universe are more valid than scientific explanations.'

   Evaluate this statement.

   In your answer you:

   - should give reasoned arguments in support of this statement
   - should give reasoned arguments to support a different point of view
   - should refer to religious arguments
   - may refer to non-religious arguments
   - should reach a justified conclusion.

   > This type of question asks you to evaluate the given statement. Remember that some religious believers may agree with this statement and some may have alternative views. Think about the different reasons that may be offered to support each viewpoint, using relevant religious teachings to support each view and showing awareness of non-religious beliefs. End your answer with a considered, overall conclusion before reading through your answer carefully to check for spelling, punctuation and grammar.

   ....
   ....
   ....
   ....
   ....
   ....
   ....
   ....
   ....
   ....
   ....
   ....
   ....
   ....
   ....
   ....
   ....
   ....
   ....

   (12 marks + 3 SPaG marks)

Please complete your answer on your own paper if you need more space.

Had a go ☐ Nearly there ☐ Nailed it! ☐

Islam

Theme B

Components 2A and 2B

Origins of the universe

1 Which **one** of the following is the word used to describe the argument that God created everything in the universe?

Put a tick (✓) in the box next to the correct answer.

A Evolution ☐
B Big Bang theory ☐
C Creation ☐
D Collision argument ☐

> Make sure you are clear about what each argument you have studied is called.

(1 mark)

2 Explain **two** religious beliefs about using science and religion to explain the origin of the universe.

Refer to sacred writings or another source of religious belief and teaching in your answer.

> Remember that some religious believers (literalists) accept that science challenges religious ideas about the origin of the universe and so may reject science. Others (non-literalists) believe science and religion can work together. You might like to use one or both viewpoints in your answer.

....

....

....

....

....

....

....

....

....

....

....

....

(5 marks)

Christianity
Theme B
Components 2A and 2B

Had a go ☐   Nearly there ☐   Nailed it! ☐

The value of the world

1 Which **one** of the following describes the religious duty given to humans to look after and care for the world?

Put a tick (✓) in the box next to the correct answer.

- A Dominion ☐
- B Stewardship ☐
- C Fossil fuels ☐
- D Environment ☐

> Look at the four options carefully. It is good revision practice to check your understanding of each term before deciding which one you think correctly answers the question.

(1 mark)

Guided

2 Explain **two** religious beliefs about the duty of humanity to care for the world.

Refer to sacred writings or another source of religious belief and teaching in your answer.

Christians believe God gave humans stewardship over the Earth, which is a responsibility to care for his creation and look after it. ....

> Two religious beliefs are described, one from Christianity and one from Islam. (You could explain two beliefs from within one religion, if you prefer.) Develop each belief fully by giving further explanation or examples. Link at least one belief to a source of religious authority, such as the Bible or the Qur'an, quoting directly or summarising in your own words.

....

....

....

....

Muslims are taught that Allah made humans khalifahs (stewards) and gave them the responsibility to care for the universe. ....

....

....

....

....

....

(5 marks)

Had a go ☐　Nearly there ☐　Nailed it! ☐

Islam

Theme B

Components 2A and 2B

The value of the world

Guided

1 'Everyone has a responsibility to care for the world.'

Evaluate this statement.

In your answer you:

- should give reasoned arguments in support of this statement
- should give reasoned arguments to support a different point of view
- should refer to religious arguments
- may refer to non-religious arguments
- should reach a justified conclusion.

> Start by offering reasons that agree with the statement – Christians and Muslims will hold similar beliefs. Complete your answer by adding any further reasons and then write a justified conclusion that is linked to the ideas you have presented in your answer. Read through your answer carefully to check for spelling, punctuation and grammar.

Many Muslims strongly agree with the statement as they believe the Qur'an is clear that Allah is the creator of the world and that it does not belong to humans. ....

....

....

....

Christians are taught that God made humans stewards of the Earth. .....

....

....

....

Another reason why religious believers may agree is ....

....

....

....

An alternative view may be from non-religious believers, who may argue that, although they do not believe a God created the universe, humans should still look after the world. ....

....

....

....

....

(12 marks + 3 SPaG marks)

Please complete your answer on your own paper if you need more space.

Christianity
Theme B
Components 2A and 2B

Had a go ☐ Nearly there ☐ Nailed it! ☐

The natural world

1. Give **two** examples of how religious believers can help care for the world.

   1 ....
   ....
   ....

   2 ....
   ....
   ....

   > To answer this question, you simply need to state two ways in which Christians can help care for the world – you don't need to develop each idea.

   (2 marks)

Guided

2. Explain **two** religious beliefs about animals being used for food.

   Refer to sacred writings or another source of religious belief and teaching in your answer.

   Many Christians believe God gave animals to humans for the purpose of food, so they do not have a problem with animals being used for food.

   ....
   ....
   ....
   ....

   > Develop the first belief outlined here by explaining the idea further. You could link it to a teaching from the Bible (for example, Genesis 9:3) by quoting directly or summarising in your own words.

   Some Christian religious texts state that humans were 'made in the image of God' and to stand apart from animals, and were given dominion over the Earth.

   ....
   ....
   ....
   ....
   ....

   > Now develop this belief by explaining further what the idea of dominion means. If you did not link your first belief to a source of religious authority, you need to do so here.

   (5 marks)

58

Had a go ☐   Nearly there ☐   Nailed it! ☐

Islam

Theme B

Components 2A and 2B

The natural world

1 'We should not eat animals.'

Evaluate this statement.

In your answer you:

- should give reasoned arguments in support of this statement
- should give reasoned arguments to support a different point of view
- should refer to religious arguments
- may refer to non-religious arguments
- should reach a justified conclusion.

> Remember that Muslims have special rules about how meat should be killed (halal). Christians accept that, although there is a responsibility to care for animals, God gave them to humans to eat. Some religious believers, however, may choose to be vegetarian. Make sure you include a range of views in your answer before coming to a reasoned conclusion. Read through your answer carefully to check for spelling, punctuation and grammar.

....
....
....
....
....
....
....
....
....
....
....
....
....
....
....
....
....
....
....

(12 marks + 3 SPaG marks)

Please complete your answer on your own paper if you need more space.

Christianity — Theme B (Components 2A and 2B)

Had a go ☐   Nearly there ☐   Nailed it! ☐

Origins of human life

1. Which **one** of the following describes the scientific theory of the development of species put forward by Charles Darwin?

   Put a tick (✓) in the box next to the correct answer.

   A Genesis ☐
   B Big Bang theory ☐
   C Evolution ☐
   D Creationism ☐

   Look at the four options carefully. It is good revision practice to check your understanding of each term before deciding which one you think correctly answers the question.

   (1 mark)

Guided

2. Explain **two** religious beliefs about the compatibility of religious and scientific views on the origins of humanity.

   Refer to sacred writings or another source of religious belief and teaching in your answer.

   Some Christians believe it is possible to accept both scientific and religious accounts of the origins of humanity. ....

   ....

   Develop the first belief outlined here by adding further explanation. You could also link it to a source of religious belief and teaching, such as the Bible, by quoting directly or summarising in your own words.

   ....

   Now add a second religious belief. This could be another Christian belief that is different from the one above or a religious belief from Islam. If you did not link the first belief to a religious source, you need to do so here.

   ....

   (5 marks)

60

Had a go ☐   Nearly there ☐   Nailed it! ☐

Islam

Theme B

Components 2A and 2B

Origins of human life

> **Guided**

1 Give **two** religious beliefs about the creation of humans.

   1 Muslims believe Adam and Hawa (Eve) were the first humans.

   ....

   2 ....

   ....

   State a second, different belief about the creation of humans.

   (2 marks)

2 Explain **two** religious beliefs about the scientific theory of evolution.

   Refer to sacred writings or another source of religious belief and teaching in your answer.

   Consider which two beliefs you could write about before you start your answer; you can include beliefs from Christianity or Islam. Develop your first belief fully before moving on to explaining your second belief. This style of question also asks you to refer to a source of religious authority, such as the Bible or the Qur'an, by either quoting directly or summarising in your own words.

   (5 marks)

Christianity — Theme B (Components 2A and 2B)

Had a go ☐   Nearly there ☐   Nailed it! ☐

Sanctity and quality of life

1 'Poor quality of life would be an acceptable reason to end a person's life.'

Evaluate this statement.

In your answer you:

- should give reasoned arguments in support of this statement
- should give reasoned arguments to support a different point of view
- should refer to religious arguments
- may refer to non-religious arguments
- should reach a justified conclusion.

> This type of question asks you to consider a range of views. You may wish to look in the Revision Guide again at pages 64 and 65 on euthanasia, which are also relevant. Think about the different religious and non-religious arguments that may be offered to support each viewpoint, referring to religious teachings where relevant. Finish with a well-considered conclusion before reading through your answer carefully to check for spelling, punctuation and grammar.

....
....
....
....
....
....
....
....
....
....
....
....
....
....
....
....
....
....
....
....

(12 marks + 3 SPaG marks)

Please complete your answer on your own paper if you need more space.

Had a go ☐   Nearly there ☐   Nailed it! ☐

Islam
Theme B
Components 2A and 2B

Sanctity and quality of life

1. Which **one** of the following is the phrase used to describe the religious belief that life is sacred because God created it?

   Put a tick (✓) in the box next to the correct answer.

   > Remember that you need to know all these phrases, so make sure you revise them.

   A Quality of life ☐
   B Sanctity of life ☐
   C Stewardship ☐
   D Right to die ☐

   (1 mark)

Guided

2. Give **two** reasons why religious believers think life is sacred.

   1 Muslims believe life is sacred because Allah created it. ....

   ....

   2 ....

   > State a second belief that is different from the first one given here.

   ....

   ....

   (2 marks)

3. Give **two** religious beliefs about quality of life.

   1 ....

   ....

   ....

   2 ....

   > Quality of life is the value or meaning a life has. Remember that it is different to sanctity of life.

   ....

   ....

   (2 marks)

Christianity — Theme B
Components 2A and 2B

Had a go ☐   Nearly there ☐   Nailed it! ☐

Abortion and euthanasia

Guided

1 Give **two** religious beliefs about abortion being wrong.

1 Some Christians believe abortion is wrong as life is a sacred gift from God. ....

2 ....

....

....

> This question simply asks you to state two different religious beliefs – you don't need to explain them. The first religious belief is given; you need to add a second one. Remember that this could be from Christianity or Islam.

(2 marks)

2 Explain **two** similar beliefs about euthanasia being wrong.

In your answer you must refer to one or more religious traditions.

....
....
....
....
....
....
....
....
....
....
....
....

> This style of question asks you to consider two similar beliefs within a religious tradition (for example, within Christianity) or across two different religious traditions (such as Christianity and Islam). Make sure you develop each belief fully by adding new information or further explanation.

(4 marks)

Had a go ☐   Nearly there ☐   Nailed it! ☐

Islam

Theme B

Components 2A and 2B

Abortion and euthanasia

> **Guided**

1 'Abortion should never be allowed.'

Evaluate this statement.

In your answer you:

- should give reasoned arguments in support of this statement
- should give reasoned arguments to support a different point of view
- should refer to religious arguments
- may refer to non-religious arguments
- should reach a justified conclusion.

> There are many views you can include on this statement – Muslim, Christian and non-religious. Make sure you develop each reason fully and come to a reasoned conclusion that is based on the arguments at the end. Read through your answer carefully to check for spelling, punctuation and grammar.

Some Muslims believe abortion is wrong and should never be allowed as all life is special and sacred because Allah created it. ....

....

....

....

However, some Christians and Muslims recognise that, although life is sacred, abortion should sometimes be allowed. ....

....

....

....

Some non-religious believers claim abortion is a personal choice and should be an option. ....

....

....

....

Overall, after considering all arguments, I believe the strongest point is given by ....

....

....

....

(12 marks + 3 SPaG marks)

Please complete your answer on your own paper if you need more space.

Christianity

Theme B — Components 2A and 2B

Had a go ☐ Nearly there ☐ Nailed it! ☐

Death and the afterlife

1. Which **one** of the following is a term used to describe the belief that there is life after death?

   Put a tick (✓) in the box next to the correct answer.

   - A Afterlife ☐
   - B Heaven ☐
   - C Hell ☐
   - D Judgement ☐

   > This style of question uses subject-specific terminology so make sure you learn your key words thoroughly. Check your understanding of each term before deciding which one you think is correct.

   (1 mark)

Guided

2. Explain **two** religious beliefs about life after death.

   Refer to sacred writings or another source of religious belief and teaching in your answer.

   Christians believe the resurrection of Jesus shows there is life after death. ....

   > Consider which two beliefs you may write about before you start your answer. You can include beliefs from Christianity or Islam. This style of question also asks you to refer to a source of religious authority, such as the Bible or the Qur'an, by either quoting directly or summarising in your own words.

   (5 marks)

Had a go ☐   Nearly there ☐   Nailed it! ☐

Islam
Theme B
Components 2A and 2B

Death and the afterlife

> **Guided**

1 'Everyone should live with awareness of the afterlife.'

Evaluate this statement.

In your answer you:

- should give reasoned arguments in support of this statement
- should give reasoned arguments to support a different point of view
- should refer to religious arguments
- may refer to non-religious arguments
- should reach a justified conclusion.

Consider a range of views on this statement and put forward arguments to support them. Make sure you develop each argument fully and include relevant religious teachings where possible. Read through your answer carefully to check for spelling, punctuation and grammar.

Belief in the afterlife is important to Muslims. They believe Allah is watching and will judge them on the way they have behaved: Surah 39:70 states that Allah is aware of every person's thoughts and actions. Muslims believe Allah's judgement determines whether they go to heaven (al-Jannah) or hell (Jahannam).

Another reason why Muslims may agree with the statement is ....

....

....

....

....

....

....

An alternative view is ....

....

....

....

....

....

....

....

(12 marks + 3 SPaG marks)

Please complete your answer on your own paper if you need more space.

Christianity Islam — Theme B — Components 2A and 2B

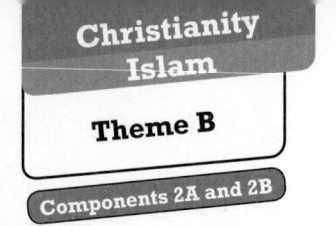

Had a go ☐   Nearly there ☐   Nailed it! ☐

Religion and life: Contrasting beliefs

1. Explain **two** similar religious beliefs about animal testing.

   In your answer you must refer to one or more religious traditions.

   > This question asks you to consider two similar beliefs within a religious tradition (for example, within Christianity) or across two different religious traditions (such as Christianity and Islam) on the topic of animal testing. Make sure you develop each belief fully by adding new information.

   ....

   (4 marks)

2. Explain **two** contrasting beliefs in contemporary British society on abortion.

   In your answer you should refer to the main religious tradition of Great Britain and one or more other religious traditions.

   > This question asks you to consider two opposing beliefs. Remember that the main religious tradition of Great Britain is Christianity. Christians hold different beliefs about this topic so you could choose to discuss two contrasting beliefs from within Christianity or you could give contrasting beliefs from Christianity and Islam.

   ....

   (4 marks)

Had a go ☐   Nearly there ☐   Nailed it! ☐

Christianity Islam

Theme B

Components 2A and 2B

Religion and life: Contrasting beliefs

Guided

1. Explain **two** similar religious beliefs about abortion.

   In your answer you should refer to the main religious tradition of Great Britain and one or more other religious traditions.

   Some Christians believe there are times when abortion, although not encouraged, is the 'lesser of two evils'.

   > This question asks you to consider two similar beliefs within a religious tradition (for example, within Christianity) or across two different religious traditions (such as Christianity and Islam) on abortion. The first belief given here is from Christianity. You need to add a second similar belief, either from another Christian denomination or from Islam. Note that both need be developed.

   ....
   ....
   ....
   ....
   ....
   ....
   ....
   ....

   (4 marks)

2. Explain **two** similar religious beliefs about euthanasia being legalised.

   In your answer you should refer to the main religious tradition of Great Britain and one or more other religious traditions.

   > Remember that many religions, including Islam and Christianity, state that euthanasia is wrong because of key religious teachings. You need to present two similar ideas, developing each one fully.

   ....
   ....
   ....
   ....
   ....
   ....
   ....
   ....
   ....

   (4 marks)

Christianity
Theme C
Components 2A and 2B

Had a go ☐ Nearly there ☐ Nailed it! ☐

The existence of God

1. Which **one** of the following is the name given to the argument that tries to prove God's existence by arguing that everything is caused by something else?

   Put a tick (✓) in the box next to the correct answer.

   A Design argument ☐
   B First Cause argument ☐
   C Existence argument ☐
   D Proving God argument ☐

   > This style of question simply asks you to identify the correct answer – it is testing your factual recall. Make sure you are clear about what each argument you have studied is called.

   (1 mark)

Guided

2. Explain **two** religious beliefs about what the Design argument proves about the nature of God.

   Refer to sacred writings or another source of religious belief and teaching in your answer.

   The Design argument tries to prove that God is omnipotent (all-powerful).

   ....

   > Develop the point in this guided answer by explaining how the Design argument tries to show that God is omnipotent. Then explain a second belief about what the Design argument proves about the nature of God. Remember to link to sacred writings in your answer for at least one of the beliefs you explain. For example, you say in your own words or quote directly from Genesis on the creation of the world.

   (5 marks)

70

Had a go ☐ Nearly there ☐ Nailed it! ☐

Islam — Theme C — Components 2A and 2B

The existence of God

Guided 1 Give **two** strengths of the Design argument in proving God's existence.

1 The Design argument supports accounts in the holy books about the creation of the universe.

....

2 ....

....

....

You simply need to state a different, second strength of the Design argument – you don't need to explain it.

(2 marks)

Guided 2 Explain **two** religious beliefs about the First Cause argument.

Refer to sacred writings or another source of religious belief and teaching in your answer.

The First Cause argument can be seen in the Islamic cosmological argument called 'the kalam', which states that as everything has a cause, the universe must have a cause. ....

....

....

....

....

....

....

....

....

....

You could answer this question from an Islamic or a Christian perspective, or you could refer to both religions. Make sure you develop each belief you present by adding new information or an explanation, and perhaps an example. Remember to link to sacred writings for at least one of the beliefs you explain.

(5 marks)

Christianity

Theme C — Components 2A and 2B

Had a go ☐ Nearly there ☐ Nailed it! ☐

Miracles

1. Give **two** examples of religious miracles.

   1 ....
   ....
   ....

   2 ....
   ....

   > The examples you give can be from one religious tradition or from both Christianity and Islam. You simply need to state the name of the miracle – you don't need to explain it.

   (2 marks)

Guided

2. Explain **two** religious beliefs about the importance of miracles.

   Refer to sacred writings or another source of religious belief and teaching in your answer.

   Christians believe miracles prove the existence of an all-powerful being who is involved within the world. ....

   ....
   ....
   ....
   ....
   ....
   ....

   > Develop each religious belief outlined in this guided answer by adding further information and examples. Remember to link at least one belief to a source of religious authority, such as the Bible or the Qur'an, by either quoting directly or summarising in your own words.

   Miracles are important to Muslims as the Qur'an makes it clear that Allah is able to perform miracles if he wants to. ....

   ....
   ....
   ....
   ....
   ....

   (5 marks)

72

Had a go ☐ Nearly there ☐ Nailed it! ☐

Islam

Theme C

Components 2A and 2B

Miracles

1. Which **one** of the following is **not** an example of a way that God reveals himself?

   Put a tick (✓) in the box next to the correct answer.

   A Miracles ☐
   B Visions ☐
   C Agnostic ☐
   D Through holy books ☐

   > Make sure you read each possible answer carefully before choosing the correct one.

   (1 mark)

> **Guided**

2. Explain **two** similar religious beliefs about the importance of miracles in proving the existence of God.

   In your answer you must refer to one or more religious traditions.

   Miracles are important to Muslims in showing that God is omnibenevolent and cares for his creation by acting to help humans. This can be seen through examples such as ....

   ....

   ....

   ....

   ....

   > For this type of question you need to identify two similar beliefs; these could be from Christianity or Islam, or from both religions. Complete this answer by developing each idea. For example, you could add more information or give examples.

   Some Christians believe miracles prove God is omniscient as he must be watching the world to be able to intervene and help humans. This can be seen in ....

   ....

   ....

   ....

   ....

   (4 marks)

73

Christianity — Theme C — Components 2A and 2B

Had a go ☐ Nearly there ☐ Nailed it! ☐

Evil and suffering

1 'It is possible to accept evil and suffering in the world and still believe in God.'

Evaluate this statement.

In your answer you:

- should give reasoned arguments in support of this statement
- should give reasoned arguments to support a different point of view
- should refer to religious arguments
- may refer to non-religious arguments
- should reach a justified conclusion.

> This type of question asks you to evaluate the given statement. Remember that some religious believers may agree with this statement and some may have alternative views. Think about the different reasons that may be offered to support each viewpoint, using relevant religious teachings throughout and showing awareness of non-religious beliefs. End your answer with a considered, overall conclusion before reading through your answer carefully to check for spelling, punctuation and grammar.

(12 marks + 3 SPaG marks)

Please complete your answer on your own paper if you need more space.

Had a go ☐   Nearly there ☐   Nailed it! ☐

Islam
Theme C
Components 2A and 2B

Evil and suffering

1. Which **one** of the following describes a person who argues that the presence of evil and suffering in the world means God cannot exist?

   Put a tick (✓) in the box next to the correct answer.

   A Compassionate ☐
   B Atheist ☐
   C Free will ☐
   D Omnibenevolent ☐

   > You just need to identify the one answer that is correct. Make sure you read the question carefully.

   (1 mark)

Guided

2. Give **two** characteristics of God that are challenged by the presence of evil and suffering in the world.

   1 It challenges the idea of God being all-loving (omnibenevolent). ....

   2 ....

   ....

   ....

   > Make sure you give two different ideas rather than two ideas that are the same (for example, saying the loving nature of God as one answer and then the idea that God is omnibenevolent as the second, as these mean the same thing).

   (2 marks)

Guided

3. Give **two** examples of how religious believers can help those who are suffering in the world.

   1 Muslims believe they can help others by doing charity work. ....

   2 ....

   ....

   ....

   > You don't need to develop any points you make.

   (2 marks)

Christianity

Theme C

Components 2A and 2B

Had a go ☐ Nearly there ☐ Nailed it! ☐

Arguments against the existence of God

Guided 1 Give **two** examples of how scientific arguments challenge belief in God.

1 The Big Bang theory offers an alternative explanation to God creating the world. ....

2 ....

....

> To complete this question, you simply need to state a second example – you don't need to develop it or explain it further.

.... **(2 marks)**

Guided 2 Explain **two** religious beliefs about how scientific argument does **not** pose a challenge to belief in God.

Refer to sacred writings or another source of religious belief and teaching in your answer.

Some Christians believe science does not pose a challenge to belief in God because science and religion together explain how the world came to exist.

> Develop the belief given here by explaining the idea further (for example, you could focus on the Big Bang theory or on evolutionary theory). Then explain a second religious belief, answering from within one religious tradition or by referring to both Christian and Muslim beliefs. Make sure you link at least one belief to a source of religious writing, by either quoting directly or summarising in your own words.

....

....

....

....

....

....

....

....

....

.... **(5 marks)**

Had a go ☐ Nearly there ☐ Nailed it! ☐

Islam — Theme C — Components 2A and 2B

Arguments against the existence of God

Guided

1. 'Arguments based on science are always a threat to the existence of God.'

   Evaluate this statement.

   In your answer you:

   - should give reasoned arguments in support of this statement
   - should give reasoned arguments to support a different point of view
   - should refer to religious arguments
   - may refer to non-religious arguments
   - should reach a justified conclusion.

   > Religious believers such as Muslims and Christians are divided on this issue so try to show this in your answer. Make sure you also include a non-religious view as well as a thoughtful conclusion at the end. Read through your answer carefully to check for spelling, punctuation and grammar.

   Some literalist Muslims may agree with the statement, arguing that all scientific explanations should be rejected because they are against Islamic teachings. ....

   ....

   ....

   ....

   ....

   ....

   Some Muslims may disagree with the statement, believing there are many similarities between the Qur'an and scientific explanations.

   ....

   ....

   ....

   ....

   ....

   ....

   ....

   (12 marks + 3 SPaG marks)

Please complete your answer on your own paper if you need more space.

Christianity
Theme C
Components 2A and 2B

Had a go ☐ Nearly there ☐ Nailed it! ☐

Special revelation: Visions

1 Which **one** of the following is **not** a type of revelation of God?

Put a tick (✓) in the box next to the correct answer.

- A Visions ☐
- B Miracles ☐
- C Scripture ☐
- D Hymns ☐

> Read the question carefully. It is asking you to identify which answer is **not** an example of revelation of God. Remember that revelation is when something is revealed about God.

(1 mark)

Guided

2 Give **two** reasons why visions are important to religious believers.

1 Visions are important to Christians because they allow messages from God to be passed on. ....

> Complete this answer by giving a second reason that is different from the first one. You simply need to state the reason – you don't need to explain it further.

2 ....

....

(2 marks)

3 Give **two** examples of miracles that religious believers may accept as proof of God's existence.

1 ....
....
....
....

> The examples you give can be from one religious tradition or from both Christianity and Islam. You simply need to state two examples that may be considered evidence for belief in God. You are not required to develop them.

2 ....

....

....

(2 marks)

Had a go ☐   Nearly there ☐   Nailed it! ☐

Islam — Theme C — Components 2A and 2B

Special revelation: Visions

1 'Visions are not a good source of revelation of God.'

Evaluate this statement.

In your answer you:

- should give reasoned arguments in support of this statement
- should give reasoned arguments to support a different point of view
- should refer to religious arguments
- may refer to non-religious arguments
- should reach a justified conclusion.

> Remember that you can include both Muslim and Christian beliefs on this statement if you wish. Some religious believers may place more emphasis on visions as a form of revelation – try to show awareness of this within the arguments you use. Read through your answer carefully to check for spelling, punctuation and grammar.

....
....
....
....
....
....
....
....
....
....
....
....
....
....
....
....
....
....
....
....

(12 marks + 3 SPaG marks)

Please complete your answer on your own paper if you need more space.

Christianity — Theme C — Components 2A and 2B

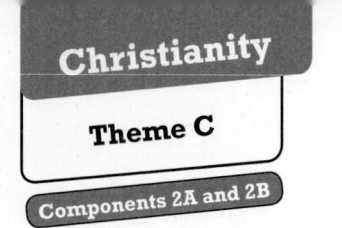

Had a go ☐   Nearly there ☐   Nailed it! ☐

General revelation

1 'Those who claim to have had revelation of God are mistaken.'

Evaluate this statement.

In your answer you:

- should give reasoned arguments in support of this statement
- should give reasoned arguments to support a different point of view
- should refer to religious arguments
- may refer to non-religious arguments
- should reach a justified conclusion.

> This statement is something a non-religious believer might argue. Consider the various religious and non-religious arguments that may be offered in support of the statement as well as to support a different point of view. Throughout your answer, back up your arguments with reference to religious teachings, where relevant. End with a justified conclusion before reading through your answer carefully to check for spelling, punctuation and grammar.

(12 marks + 3 SPaG marks)

Please complete your answer on your own paper if you need more space.

Had a go ☐ Nearly there ☐ Nailed it! ☐

Islam — Theme C — Components 2A and 2B

General revelation

1 Which **one** of the following is **not** an example of general revelation, when God is revealed indirectly?

Put a tick (✓) in the box next to the correct answer.

A Nature ☐
B Miracles ☐
C Scripture (holy books) ☐
D Messengers ☐

Revise the difference between special revelation and general revelation so you are able to choose the correct answer to this question.

(1 mark)

Guided

2 Give **two** examples of general revelation.

1 Through prophets such as Muhammad.
   ....

2 ....
   ....
   ....

The first example given here is correct for Muslims: revelation of God is seen indirectly through prophets such as Muhammad. Add a second relevant example for either Muslims or Christians.

(2 marks)

3 Give **two** problems about general revelation.

1 ....
   ....
   ....

2 ....
   ....
   ....

Make sure you understand this question correctly. It is asking for reasons why there may be a problem with general revelation. Identify two correct answers.

(2 marks)

81

Christianity Islam
Theme C
Components 2A and 2B

Had a go ☐   Nearly there ☐   Nailed it! ☐

The existence of God and revelation: Contrasting beliefs

Guided 1 Explain **two** similar religious beliefs about the importance of nature as general revelation.

In your answer you must refer to one or more religious traditions.

Many Christians believe nature provides good evidence of God as they accept that God created the world and believe the complexity of the world shows God's power and loving nature. Some Christians may argue that the Design argument provides good support for nature as general revelation because ....

....

.... **(4 marks)**

> This question asks you to consider two similar beliefs within a religious tradition (for example, within Christianity) or across two different religious traditions (such as Christianity and Islam). Complete the first part of this answer and then add a second belief. Make sure you develop each belief fully.

Guided 2 Explain **two** contrasting beliefs in contemporary British society about visions proving the existence of God.

In your answer you should refer to the main religious tradition of Great Britain and one or more other religious traditions.

Some Muslims accept that visions happen but do not place great emphasis on them in proving that Allah is real or confirming his characteristics of omnipotence and omnibenevolence. Rather, they place greater emphasis on other sources of revelation of Allah, such as the Qur'an, which is seen as direct revelation given to Muhammad, or the prophets themselves, who gave important messages to humanity. ....

....

....

....

.... **(4 marks)**

> This question asks you to consider two opposing beliefs. Remember that the main religious tradition of Great Britain is Christianity. You could choose to discuss two contrasting beliefs from within Christianity, or you could give contrasting beliefs from Christianity and Islam. This guided answer gives a Muslim belief in response to the question. Complete it by adding a contrasting belief from Christianity.

Had a go ☐ Nearly there ☐ Nailed it! ☐

Christianity / Islam — Theme C — Components 2A and 2B

The existence of God and revelation: Contrasting beliefs

1. Explain **two** contrasting beliefs in contemporary British society about miracles.

   In your answer you should refer to the main religious tradition of Great Britain and non-religious beliefs.

   > This question asks you to consider two opposing beliefs – one from the main religious tradition of Great Britain (Christianity) and one non-religious belief. Make sure the beliefs you choose are contrasting, which means they should express completely different viewpoints.

   ....

   ....

   ....

   ....

   ....

   ....

   ....

   ....

   (4 marks)

Guided

2. Explain **two** contrasting beliefs in contemporary British society about nature providing evidence of God's existence.

   In your answer you should refer to the main religious tradition of Great Britain and non-religious beliefs.

   > This question asks you to consider two opposing beliefs – one from the main religious tradition of Great Britain (Christianity) and one non-religious belief. A non-religious explanation is given here. You need to complete the answer by giving a contrasting view from a Christian perspective.

   Many non-religious believers claim that nature does not provide evidence of God's existence. They may argue that the universe can be explained by scientific theories such as the Big Bang and evolution. They may not believe nature shows what God is like; they may accept that the world came about by chance rather than on the intervention of a divine being. Indeed, they may argue that God does not exist.

   ....

   ....

   ....

   ....

   ....

   ....

   (4 marks)

Christianity — Theme D — Components 2A and 2B

Had a go ☐   Nearly there ☐   Nailed it! ☐

Peace and justice, forgiveness and reconciliation

Guided

1 Give **two** religious beliefs that show justice is important.

  1 Christians believe God is just, so humans should be too. ....

  2 ....

  ....

  ....

  Complete the answer by giving a second reason, different from the first one given here. You simply need to state the reason – you don't need to develop it. You can answer from just one religious tradition or from both Christianity and Islam.

  (2 marks)

2 Explain **two** religious beliefs about forgiveness.

  Refer to sacred writings or another source of religious belief and teaching in your answer.

  ....

  Consider which two beliefs you could write about before you start your answer; you can include beliefs from Christianity or Islam. Remember that forgiveness is an important idea to Christians as it was taught by Jesus and can be seen in many of his teachings. Develop your first belief fully before moving on to explaining your second belief. This style of question also asks you to refer to a source of religious authority, such as the Bible or the Qur'an, by either quoting directly or summarising in your own words.

  (5 marks)

84

Had a go ☐   Nearly there ☐   Nailed it! ☐

Islam

Theme D

Components 2A and 2B

Peace and justice, forgiveness and reconciliation

1 'If everyone followed a religion in the world, there would be peace.'

Evaluate this statement.

In your answer you:

- should give reasoned arguments in support of this statement
- should give reasoned arguments to support a different point of view
- should refer to religious arguments
- may refer to non-religious arguments
- should reach a justified conclusion.

> Many arguments can be used to agree and disagree with the above statement – you may find it helpful to jot some down before you write your answer. Think about religious teachings on peace and the importance of ideas of reconciliation and forgiveness. Also, some people may view religion as being part of the problem. Use relevant religious teachings to support each argument and show awareness of non-religious beliefs. End with a considered, overall conclusion before reading through your answer carefully to check for spelling, punctuation and grammar.

....
....
....
....
....
....
....
....
....
....
....
....
....
....
....
....
....

(12 marks + 3 SPaG marks)

Please complete your answer on your own paper if you need more space.

Christianity

Theme D

Components 2A and 2B

Had a go ☐ Nearly there ☐ Nailed it! ☐

Violence and terrorism

1. Which **one** of the following is a term used to describe the use of violence and threats to try and intimidate others and cause fear?

   Put a tick (✓) in the box next to the correct answer.

   A War ☐
   B Terrorism ☐
   C Defence ☐
   D Retaliation ☐

   > This style of question simply asks you to identify the correct answer – it is testing your factual recall. Look at the four options carefully before deciding which one you think correctly answers the question.

   (1 mark)

Guided

2. Give **two** reasons why religious believers do not support terrorism.

   1 Many Christians believe acts of violence against people, such as terrorism, are wrong because God created life so it is sacred. ....

   > This question asks you to state two different reasons – you don't need to explain them. One reason is given here; you need to provide a second, different reason. This could be from a Christian or an Islamic perspective.

   2 ....
   ....
   ....

   (2 marks)

3. Give **two** religious beliefs about the use of violence.

   1 ....
   ....
   ....

   > The majority of religious believers don't support the use of violence; however, some religious believers do support the use of violence in certain circumstances. You need to state two different religious beliefs. You could answer from within one religious tradition or by giving beliefs from both Christianity and Islam.

   2 ....
   ....
   ....

   (2 marks)

Had a go ☐   Nearly there ☐   Nailed it! ☐

Islam — Theme D — Components 2A and 2B

Violence and terrorism

Guided

1. Explain **two** similar religious beliefs about the use of violence.

   In your answer you must refer to one or more religious traditions.

   Muslims believe using violence is wrong because Islam is a religion of peace. ....

   Muslims believe Allah is merciful and forgiving, therefore

   > Two similar religious beliefs about violence, both from Islam, are given here. To complete the answer, you need to develop each belief by adding more information and detail.

   ....

   ....

   ....

   ....

   ....

   ....

   (4 marks)

2. Explain **two** religious beliefs about terrorism.

   Refer to sacred writings or another source of religious belief and teaching in your answer.

   > Make sure you link at least one of the beliefs you present to a source of religious authority, such as the Bible or the Qur'an.

   ....

   ....

   ....

   ....

   ....

   ....

   ....

   ....

   ....

   ....

   (5 marks)

Christianity — Theme D — Components 2A and 2B

Had a go ☐   Nearly there ☐   Nailed it! ☐

War and Just War theory

1 'There is never a need to go to war.'

Evaluate this statement.

In your answer you:

- should give reasoned arguments in support of this statement
- should give reasoned arguments to support a different point of view
- should refer to religious arguments
- may refer to non-religious arguments
- should reach a justified conclusion.

> This type of question asks you to evaluate the given statement. Remember that some religious believers may agree with the statement and some may have alternative views. Think about the different reasons that may be offered to support each viewpoint, using relevant religious teachings to support each argument and showing awareness of non-religious beliefs. End your answer with a considered, overall conclusion before reading through your answer carefully to check for spelling, punctuation and grammar.

(12 marks + 3 SPaG marks)

Please complete your answer on your own paper if you need more space.

Had a go ☐   Nearly there ☐   Nailed it! ☐

Islam — Theme D — Components 2A and 2B

War and Just War theory

1. Which **one** of the following describes a set of rules for fighting in a way that is acceptable to God?

   Put a tick (✓) in the box next to the correct answer.

   A Pacifism ☐
   B Reconciliation ☐
   C Terrorism ☐
   D Just war ☐

   > This style of question simply asks you to identify the correct answer – it is testing your factual recall. Each answer is a term you need to know, so revise them thoroughly before identifying the correct answer.

   (1 mark)

2. Give **two** religious responses about war **not** being justified.

   1 ....

   2 ....

   > Make sure the two responses you give are different.

   (2 marks)

Guided

3. Give **two** religious beliefs about war being acceptable.

   1 Some Muslims believe war may be necessary to achieve peace, but only as a last resort after all peaceful methods have been tried first. ....

   2 ....

   > Remember that Just War theory gives a list of rules for when and how war can be justified. You could include some of these in your answer.

   (2 marks)

89

Christianity — Theme D — Components 2A and 2B

Had a go ☐ Nearly there ☐ Nailed it! ☐

Holy war

Guided 1 Give **two** religious teachings about holy war.

1 Christians generally believe war is wrong as the Bible teaches messages of peace between all people. ....

> One religious teaching is given – you need to give a second, different teaching. This can be from either Christianity or Islam.

2 ....
....
....

(2 marks)

Guided 2 Explain **two** religious beliefs about holy war being acceptable.

Refer to sacred writings or another source of religious belief and teaching in your answer.

Some Christians believe a few passages from the Old Testament in the Bible which suggest that war may sometimes be the right action to take.
....
....

> There are specific conditions when religious believers such as Christians or Muslims may support war. You could choose to show an awareness of these within the beliefs you present. Make sure you give two different beliefs, developing each fully with explanation and examples. You also need to link at least one belief to a source of religious writing, by either quoting directly or summarising in your own words.

....
....
....
....

In the past, such as during the Crusades in the Middle Ages, Christians fought in holy wars because they believed God wanted them to defend Christian holy sites from other religions. ....
....
....
....
....
....

(5 marks)

Had a go ☐ Nearly there ☐ Nailed it! ☐

Islam

Theme D

Components 2A and 2B

Holy war

1 'Holy war is no different to any other type of war.'

Evaluate this statement.

In your answer you:

- should give reasoned arguments in support of this statement
- should give reasoned arguments to support a different point of view
- should refer to religious arguments
- may refer to non-religious arguments
- should reach a justified conclusion.

> Start your answer by giving reasons to support the statement – this could be from a religious or a non-religious viewpoint. Remember that you can include Christian and Islamic arguments but make sure you develop each one fully. Read through your answer carefully to check for spelling, punctuation and grammar.

....
....
....
....
....
....
....
....
....
....
....
....
....
....
....
....
....
....
....

(12 marks + 3 SPaG marks)

Please complete your answer on your own paper if you need more space.

Christianity

Theme D — Components 2A and 2B

Had a go ☐ Nearly there ☐ Nailed it! ☐

Pacifism

1 Which **one** of the following is a term used to describe the belief that any use of violence is wrong?

Put a tick (✓) in the box next to the correct answer.

- A Justice ☐
- B Nuclear weapons ☐
- C Forgiveness ☐
- D Pacifism ☐

> This style of question simply asks you to identify the correct answer. Some words given in multiple-choice questions have similar meanings, so think carefully about what each one means before you respond.

(1 mark)

Guided

2 Explain **two** religious beliefs about supporting pacifism.

Refer to sacred writings or another source of religious belief and teaching in your answer.

Some Christians support pacifism because they believe that, as God created all humans, there is a part of God in every human and so they should oppose anything that could harm people, including violence. ....

> Some Christians, such as Quakers, choose to be pacifists. This question asks you to explain two religious beliefs that would support a person in becoming a pacifist. Remember to link at least one belief to a source of religious authority, by either quoting directly or summarising in your own words. Remember that Muslims are not pacifists, so you need to consider Christian teachings of peace in your answer.

(5 marks)

Had a go ☐ Nearly there ☐ Nailed it! ☐

Islam

Theme D

Components 2A and 2B

Pacifism

1 Which **one** of the following is an example of pacifism?

   Put a tick (✓) in the box next to the correct answer.

   A Fighting ☐
   B Guerrilla warfare ☐
   C Holy war ☐
   D Peaceful protest with no violence ☐

   > This style of question simply asks you to identify the correct answer – it is testing your factual recall. Look at the four options carefully before deciding which one you think correctly answers the question.

   (1 mark)

2 Give **two** religious beliefs about pacifism.

   1 ....
   ....
   ....

   > Remember that you can give beliefs from either Christianity or Islam. You simply need to state two beliefs – you don't need to explain them.

   2 ....
   ....
   ....

   (2 marks)

3 Give **two** reasons why religious believers support pacifism.

   1 ....
   ....
   ....

   2 ....

   > This question is asking for reasons why religious believers may support non-violence (not general beliefs about pacifism). Read every question carefully before you decide on your answer.

   ....
   ....

   (2 marks)

93

Christianity — Theme D (Components 2A and 2B)

Had a go ☐ Nearly there ☐ Nailed it! ☐

Religion as a cause of conflict

1 Give **two** reasons why religious believers do **not** support weapons of mass destruction (WMD).

1 ....

....

....

2 ....

....

> Remember that WMD are not supported by religious believers – state two different reasons why they hold this view.

(2 marks)

2 'Weapons of mass destruction can never be justified.'

Evaluate this statement.

In your answer you:

- should give reasoned arguments in support of this statement
- should give reasoned arguments to support a different point of view
- should refer to religious arguments
- may refer to non-religious arguments
- should reach a justified conclusion.

> Remember that religious believers are unlikely to support the use of WMD. However, there may be both religious and non-religious arguments about the benefits of having these weapons as a deterrent. Read through your answer carefully to check for spelling, punctuation and grammar.

....

....

....

....

....

....

....

....

....

....

....

(12 marks + 3 SPaG marks)

Please complete your answer on your own paper if you need more space.

Had a go ☐   Nearly there ☐   Nailed it! ☐

Islam
Theme D
Components 2A and 2B

Religion as a cause of conflict

1. Which **one** of the following is the term used to describe nuclear weapons?

   Put a tick (✓) in the box next to the correct answer.

   A Weapons of mass destruction ☐
   B Conventional warfare ☐
   C Holy war ☐
   D Peaceful protest with no violence ☐

   This style of question simply asks you to identify the correct answer – it is testing your factual recall. Look at the four options carefully before deciding which one you think correctly answers the question.

   (1 mark)

Guided

2. Explain **two** contrasting religious beliefs in contemporary society about weapons of mass destruction.

   In your answer you should refer to the main religious tradition of Great Britain and one or more other religious traditions.

   Some Christians recognise the value of having WMD as a deterrent to avoid wars starting and conflicts escalating into war. ....

   The main religious tradition of Great Britain is Christianity. You can contrast this by using another belief from within Christianity or by using Islam, as shown in this example. Complete each explanation.

   ....

   ....

   ....

   ....

   ....

   ....

   ....

   Some Muslims believe WMD are wrong, even as a deterrent, because

   ....

   ....

   ....

   ....

   ....

   (4 marks)

Christianity

Theme D

Components 2A and 2B

Had a go ☐   Nearly there ☐   Nailed it! ☐

Religion and peacemaking

1 Which **one** of the following is the absence of war, described as a state of harmony between people in society?

   Put a tick (✓) in the box next to the correct answer.

   A Pacifism ☐
   B Violence ☐
   C Peace ☐
   D Retaliation ☐

   > Look at the four options carefully. It is good revision practice to check your understanding of each term before deciding which one you think correctly answers the question.

   (1 mark)

2 Give **two** ways religious believers may help victims of war.

   1 ....
   ....
   ....

   > This type of question simply asks you to state two different examples – you don't need to provide further information about them.

   2 ....
   ....
   ....

   (2 marks)

3 Give **two** examples of religious believers who have worked for peace.

   1 ....
   ....
   ....

   > You do not need to provide information about how the people have worked for peace in this style of question. Just state two different examples – they can be from Christianity or Islam.

   2 ....
   ....
   ....

   (2 marks)

Had a go ☐ Nearly there ☐ Nailed it! ☐

Islam — Theme D — Components 2A and 2B

Religion and peacemaking

1 'The best way to help victims of war is through charitable organisations.'

Evaluate this statement.

In your answer you:

- should give reasoned arguments in support of this statement
- should give reasoned arguments to support a different point of view
- should refer to religious arguments
- may refer to non-religious arguments
- should reach a justified conclusion.

> Start your answer by giving reasons to support the statement. This could be from a religious or a non-religious viewpoint. You can include Christian and Islamic arguments, but make sure you develop each one fully. Refer to religious sources throughout and remember to check your answer carefully for spelling, punctuation and grammar.

....

(12 marks + 3 SPaG marks)

Please complete your answer on your own paper if you need more space.

Christianity Islam — Theme D — Components 2A and 2B

Had a go ☐   Nearly there ☐   Nailed it! ☐

Religion, peace and conflict: Contrasting beliefs

Guided

1 Explain **two** similar religious beliefs about the use of violence being wrong.

In your answer you must refer to one or more religious traditions.

Many Christians believe the use of violence is wrong, as Christianity has many teachings on peace. Some Christians choose to be pacifist because they believe they are following Jesus' teachings by doing so. ……………………………………………

> This question asks you to consider two similar beliefs within a religious tradition (for example, within Christianity) or across two different religious traditions (such as Christianity and Islam). Complete the first part of this answer, which explains a Christian belief, and then add a second belief. Can you give a similar belief from Islam, explaining why Muslims hold the same view? Make sure you develop each belief fully.

……………………………………………………………………………………………………
……………………………………………………………………………………………………
……………………………………………………………………………………………………
……………………………………………………………………………………………………
……………………………………………………………………………………………………
……………………………………………………………………………………………………
……………………………………………………………………………………………………

(4 marks)

2 Explain **two** contrasting beliefs in contemporary British society about pacifism.

In your answer you should refer to the main religious tradition of Great Britain and one or more other religious traditions.

……………………………………………………………
……………………………………………………………
……………………………………………………………

> This question asks you to consider two opposing beliefs, one of which is from the main religious tradition of Great Britain (Christianity). You could choose to discuss two contrasting beliefs from within Christianity or contrasting beliefs from Christianity and Islam. Remember that Islam is not traditionally a pacifist religion.

……………………………………………………………………………………………………
……………………………………………………………………………………………………
……………………………………………………………………………………………………
……………………………………………………………………………………………………
……………………………………………………………………………………………………
……………………………………………………………………………………………………

(4 marks)

Had a go ☐ Nearly there ☐ Nailed it! ☐

Christianity Islam
Theme D
Components 2A and 2B

Religion, peace and conflict: Contrasting beliefs

1. Explain **two** similar religious beliefs about pacifism.

   In your answer you must refer to one or more religious traditions.

   > For this type of question you need to identify two similar beliefs; these could be from Christianity or Islam, or from both religions.

   ....
   ....
   ....
   ....
   ....
   ....
   ....
   ....
   ....

   (4 marks)

> Guided

2. Explain **two** contrasting beliefs in contemporary British society about the use of violence in protests.

   In your answer you should refer to the main religious tradition of Great Britain and one or more other religious traditions.

   > This question asks you to consider two opposing beliefs, one of which must be from the main religious tradition of Great Britain (Christianity). You could discuss contrasting beliefs from within Christianity, or from Christianity and Islam. A belief from each religion is given here. Can you develop each one fully?

   Many Christians believe violent protest is wrong because the Bible teaches that we should work for peace and reconciliation between people. ....
   ....
   ....
   ....

   Some Muslims believe the use of violence may sometimes be justified when protesting in order to secure peace in the long term. ....
   ....
   ....
   ....

   (4 marks)

Christianity
Theme E
Components 2A and 2B

Had a go ☐ Nearly there ☐ Nailed it! ☐

Good and evil intentions and actions

1. Which **one** of the following is a term used to describe something or someone considered morally wrong or wicked?

    Put a tick (✓) in the box next to the correct answer.

    A Evil   ☐
    B Good   ☐
    C Crime   ☐
    D Murder   ☐

    > Look at the four options carefully. It is good revision practice to check your understanding of each term before deciding which one you think correctly answers the question.

    (1 mark)

Guided

2. Give **two** religious beliefs about the importance of good actions.

    1 Christians believe good actions will allow them to be rewarded in the afterlife by God. ....

    2 ....

    > You can answer this question from a Christian or a Muslim perspective. One belief is given here; you need to add a second, different religious belief.

    (2 marks)

3. Give **two** religious beliefs about suffering.

    1 ....

    2 ....

    > This type of question simply asks you to state two different examples – you don't need to explain them further. Many religious believers recognise that it is wrong to cause suffering to others, yet they also recognise that sometimes good can come from suffering. You could use some of these ideas in your answer.

    (2 marks)

Had a go ☐   Nearly there ☐   Nailed it! ☐

Islam

Theme E

Components 2A and 2B

Good and evil intentions and actions

1 'A person's intentions are just as important as their actions.'

Evaluate this statement.

In your answer you:

- should give reasoned arguments in support of this statement
- should give reasoned arguments to support a different point of view
- should refer to religious arguments
- may refer to non-religious arguments
- should reach a justified conclusion.

> This type of question asks you to evaluate the given statement. Remember that some religious believers may agree with the statement and some may have alternative views. Think about the different reasons that may be offered to support each viewpoint, with reference to religious teachings and non-religious arguments. End with a justified conclusion before checking your answer carefully for spelling, punctuation and grammar.

....
....
....
....
....
....
....
....
....
....
....
....
....
....
....
....
....
....

(12 marks + 3 SPaG marks)

Please complete your answer on your own paper if you need more space.

Christianity — Theme E (Components 2A and 2B)

Had a go ☐ Nearly there ☐ Nailed it! ☐

Reasons for crime

Guided

1. 'We should help those who turn to crime rather than punish them.'

   Evaluate this statement.

   In your answer you:

   - should give reasoned arguments in support of this statement
   - should give reasoned arguments to support a different point of view
   - should refer to religious arguments
   - may refer to non-religious arguments
   - should reach a justified conclusion.

   > This type of question asks you to evaluate the given statement. Remember that some religious believers may agree with this statement and some may have alternative views. Think about the different reasons to support each viewpoint, using religious teachings where relevant and showing awareness of non-religious beliefs. End with a considered conclusion before reading through your answer carefully to check for spelling, punctuation and grammar.

   Some religious believers may believe that people sometimes turn to crime for understandable reasons and therefore deserve our support.

   For example, ...

   ....

   ....

   ....

   Some Christians and Muslims would disagree with the statement as they believe all crime requires fair punishment to achieve justice — so the victim gains retribution and the criminal can reform. ....

   ....

   ....

   ....

   ....

   After considering all the arguments for and against this statement, my conclusion is ....

   ....

   ....

   ....

   ....

   ....

   (12 marks + 3 SPaG marks)

   Please complete your answer on your own paper if you need more space.

Had a go ☐ Nearly there ☐ Nailed it! ☐

Islam

Theme E

Components 2A and 2B

Reasons for crime

Guided 1 Give **two** reasons why punishment is important to religious believers.

1 Many Muslims and Christians see punishment as important because a key purpose of punishment is to bring about a peaceful society as they believe this is what Allah/God intends for the world. ....

2 ....
....
....

One reason is given here. You need to add another one, either Christian or Muslim, making sure it is different to the first one.

(2 marks)

Guided 2 Explain **two** religious beliefs about crime.

Refer to sacred writings or another source of religious belief and teaching in your answer.

Muslims believe crime is a distraction from Allah and therefore wrong. ....

This question asks for religious views on the issue of crime. Remember that there are many teachings that can be used to relate to this, so make sure you include them in your answer.

....
....
....
....
....
....

Muslims believe they have a duty to help those who are affected by crime.

....
....
....
....
....

(5 marks)

Christianity
Theme E — Components 2A and 2B

Had a go ☐ Nearly there ☐ Nailed it! ☐

Types of crime

1 Which **one** of the following is a term used to describe a crime committed because of prejudice against a person (for example, assaulting a person because they are homosexual or Asian)?

Put a tick (✓) in the box next to the correct answer.

- **A** Theft ☐
- **B** Evil ☐
- **C** Murder ☐
- **D** Hate crime ☐

> This style of question simply asks you to identify the correct answer. Some words given in multiple-choice questions have similar meanings, so think carefully about what each one means before you respond.

(1 mark)

Guided

2 Give **two** reasons why religious believers hold the view that murder is wrong.

1 Christians believe murder is against one of the Ten Commandments, which says 'You shall not kill.' ....

2 ....

....

....

> This question simply asks you to state two different reasons – you don't need to explain them. Here, you need to give a second reason why religious believers (Christians or Muslims) believe murder is wrong.

(2 marks)

3 Give **two** examples of religious rules that criminals break.

1 ....

....

....

2 ....

....

....

> Think about the crimes people commit and then identify two different religious rules that are broken through those crimes. For example, you could think about the rules given in the Ten Commandments or the Qur'an. Remember that you only need to state the rules – you don't need to explain them.

(2 marks)

Had a go ☐ Nearly there ☐ Nailed it! ☐

Islam

Theme E

Components 2A and 2B

Types of crime

Guided 1 'Hate crimes deserve the most severe punishments.'

Evaluate this statement.

In your answer you:

- should give reasoned arguments in support of this statement
- should give reasoned arguments to support a different point of view
- should refer to religious arguments
- may refer to non-religious arguments
- should reach a justified conclusion.

> A hate crime is a crime committed because of an opinion held against a group of people. For example, Muslims may face Islamophobia and be targeted unfairly: that is an example of a hate crime. End with a considered conclusion before reading through your answer carefully to check for spelling, punctuation and grammar.

Some Muslims may agree with the statement as Muslims in Britain have been the victims of hate crimes in recent times. ....

....

....

....

....

Some Muslims may argue that murder is a more serious crime than hate crime and so deserves the strongest punishment. They may argue that all crimes require appropriate and just punishments and more serious crimes require more severe punishments to ensure justice is served.

....

....

....

....

Overall, to conclude ....

....

....

....

....

(12 marks + 3 SPaG marks)

Please complete your answer on your own paper if you need more space.

105

Christianity — Theme E
Components 2A and 2B

Had a go ☐ Nearly there ☐ Nailed it! ☐

Punishment

Guided 1 Give **two** aims of punishment.

1 One aim of punishment is for criminals to realise what they have done wrong and to change their behaviour. ....

2 ....
....
....

> This first part of the answer correctly identifies one aim of punishment: reformation. It is a good idea to learn the key terms for the four aims of punishment, as well be able to explain what they mean. Complete the answer by giving a second example. Remember that you only need to state it; you don't need to explain it.

(2 marks)

Guided 2 Explain **two** religious beliefs about the importance of punishments for criminals.

Refer to sacred writings or another source of religious belief and teaching in your answer.

Christians believe it is important for criminals to be punished when they have committed a crime as they believe God is just and fair and so they should try to be too. Punishing a criminal fairly for a crime allows for justice, which helps the victim feel the criminal has 'paid' for their actions.

> Develop this answer by adding further information and examples from Christianity. For example, you could refer to Jesus' teachings about forgiving others when they do wrong and helping them. This style of question also asks you to refer to a source of religious authority, such as the Bible, for at least one of the beliefs, by either quoting directly or summarising in your own words.

....
....
....

Christians believe criminals should be given the opportunity to reform themselves and change their behaviour. ....
....
....
....
....

(5 marks)

Had a go ☐   Nearly there ☐   Nailed it! ☐

Islam — Theme E — Components 2A and 2B

Punishment

1. Which **one** of the following is **not** an aim of punishment?

   Put a tick (✓) in the box next to the correct answer.

   A Reformation ☐
   B Protection ☐
   C Deterrence ☐
   D Revenge ☐

   You need to know all the aims of punishment and the correct terms for them. Check your understanding of each term in the possible answers.

   (1 mark)

Guided

2. Explain **two** religious beliefs about the reformation of criminals.

   Refer to sacred writings or another source of religious belief and teaching in your answer.

   This question asks specifically about one aim of punishment – reformation – which is giving a criminal the opportunity to change their behaviour. Complete this answer with further information and examples, making sure you link at least one to a source of religious authority and teaching, such as the Qur'an or the Bible.

   Muslims believe the reformation of criminals is a key aim of punishment as Islam teaches about the importance of giving people a second chance and allowing them to change their behaviour. ....

   ....

   ....

   ....

   ....

   Christianity teaches that the reformation of criminals is important. Christians are taught to follow the example of Jesus in demonstrating agape love towards criminals and giving them time to reform. ....

   ....

   ....

   ....

   ....

   (5 marks)

Christianity — Theme E
Components 2A and 2B

The treatment of criminals

1 'Criminals should have the same rights and treatment as others in society.'

Evaluate this statement.

In your answer you:

- should give reasoned arguments in support of this statement
- should give reasoned arguments to support a different point of view
- should refer to religious arguments
- may refer to non-religious arguments
- should reach a justified conclusion.

> This type of question asks you to evaluate the given statement, which can result in many different views. Some people – both religious and non-religious – may argue that, although criminals have done wrong, they still deserve human rights and fair treatment. Others may believe that, because criminals have done wrong, they deserve to be treated differently and to have some of their rights and freedoms taken away. Show an awareness of these differing views and arguments within your answer, with reference to religious sources. End with a considered overall conclusion before reading through your answer carefully to check for spelling, punctuation and grammar.

Had a go ☐ Nearly there ☐ Nailed it! ☐

(12 marks + 3 SPaG marks)

Please complete your answer on your own paper if you need more space.

Had a go ☐ Nearly there ☐ Nailed it! ☐

Islam

Theme E

The treatment of criminals

Components 2A and 2B

1. Which **one** of the following is an example of a punishment that may seem fair for a criminal who has committed a serious crime?

   Put a tick (✓) in the box next to the correct answer.

   A Taking away food ☐
   B Imprisonment ☐
   C Stopping them having friends ☐
   D Taking away medical care ☐

   > Read through the four options carefully before deciding which one correctly answers the question. Here, the four options are all examples of human rights relating to the treatment of criminals.

   (1 mark)

> Guided

2. Explain **two** religious beliefs about the treatment of criminals.

   Refer to sacred writings or another source of religious belief and teaching in your answer.

   Most Muslims believe criminals should be treated with dignity and still have their basic human rights respected. ....

   > Two ideas are identified. You need to develop each one and link at least one of them to a teaching from a source of authority. Remember that, when answering a question like this, you can give both reasons from the same religion or one from Christianity and one from Islam, as is shown here.

   ....

   ....

   ....

   ....

   Christians believe criminals should have a fair trial. ....

   ....

   ....

   ....

   ....

   ....

   ....

   (5 marks)

109

Christianity

Theme E — Components 2A and 2B

Had a go ☐   Nearly there ☐   Nailed it! ☐

Forgiveness

Guided 1. Give **two** reasons why religious believers feel it is important to forgive criminals.

1 Forgiving someone when they have done something wrong allows for reconciliation, which is an important teaching in Christianity. ....

2 ....
....
....

> The first answer shows an awareness that reconciliation is important. You need to give a second, different reason to answer this question. Remember that you only need to state it; you don't need to explain it.

(2 marks)

Guided 2. Explain **two** similar religious beliefs about forgiving criminals.

In your answer you must refer to one or more religious traditions.

Christians believe it is important to forgive criminals because Jesus died on the cross to bring forgiveness and reconciliation between God and humanity. ....

> This answer gives two religious beliefs from Christianity, which each show why it is important to forgive criminals. Develop each reason fully by giving further information or explanation, or appropriate examples.

....
....
....

Christians believe the Lord's Prayer teaches that we should forgive criminals as we would like to be forgiven. ....

....
....
....
....

(4 marks)

110

Had a go ☐   Nearly there ☐   Nailed it! ☐

Islam

Theme E

Components 2A and 2B

Forgiveness

1. Which **one** of the following aims of punishment is the idea of forgiveness linked to?

   Put a tick (✓) in the box next to the correct answer.

   A Reformation ☐
   B Vindication ☐
   C Deterrence ☐
   D Protection of people in society ☐

   > Remember that forgiveness is about a criminal realising what they have done is wrong and being sorry for it before everybody involved is given the chance to be able to move on with their lives.

   (1 mark)

2. Explain **two** religious beliefs about forgiveness.

   Refer to sacred writings or another source of religious belief and teaching in your answer.

   > This question asks you to explain two religious beliefs about forgiveness. You could answer from a Muslim or a Christian perspective, or refer to both religions. Remember to link at least one belief to a source of religious teaching, such as the Qur'an or the Bible.

   ....

   ....

   ....

   ....

   ....

   ....

   ....

   ....

   ....

   ....

   ....

   ....

   ....

   ....

   (5 marks)

Christianity — Theme E — Components 2A and 2B

Had a go ☐ Nearly there ☐ Nailed it! ☐

The death penalty

1. Which **one** of the following is another way of referring to the death penalty?

   Put a tick (✓) in the box next to the correct answer.

   A Corporal punishment ☐
   B Capital punishment ☐
   C Community service order ☐
   D Young offenders ☐

   Check your understanding of each term before deciding which one correctly answers the question.

   (1 mark)

Guided 2. Give **two** purposes of the death penalty.

   1. The death penalty is used to deter other criminals from committing the same crime.

   2. ....

   A purpose is the reason why something is done. You need to give two different reasons why the death penalty may be used. Remember that you only need to state your answer; you don't need to explain it.

   (2 marks)

Guided 3. Explain **two** contrasting beliefs in contemporary British society about the death penalty being used.

   In your answer you should refer to the main religious tradition of Great Britain and one or more other religious traditions.

   Two contrasting beliefs are given. Develop each one by adding further detail and examples.

   ....

   (4 marks)

112

Had a go ☐   Nearly there ☐   Nailed it! ☐

Islam

Theme E

Components 2A and 2B

The death penalty

Guided

1   'The death penalty should only be used for the most serious of crimes.'

Evaluate this statement.

In your answer you:

- should give reasoned arguments in support of this statement
- should give reasoned arguments to support a different point of view
- should refer to religious arguments
- may refer to non-religious arguments
- should reach a justified conclusion.

> Continue this guided answer by explaining what the Qur'an and Hadith say about the death penalty. Then offer more views in support of the statement, which could be from Islam or Christianity, or non-religious arguments. Next, consider alternative responses to the statement before ending with a justified conclusion based on the arguments you have presented. Remember to check your answer carefully for spelling, punctuation and grammar.

Some Muslims would agree with the statement, as both the Qur'an and Hadith offer support for the death penalty for the most serious crimes.

....

....

....

....

....

....

....

....

....

....

....

....

....

....

....

....

....

(12 marks + 3 SPaG marks)

Please complete your answer on your own paper if you need more space.

Christianity / Islam — Theme E — Components 2A and 2B

Had a go ☐ Nearly there ☐ Nailed it! ☐

Religion, crime and punishment: Contrasting beliefs

Guided

1. Explain **two** similar religious beliefs about the use of corporal punishment being wrong.

   In your answer you must refer to one or more religious traditions.

   Many Christians believe the use of corporal punishment goes against the teaching of the sanctity of human life. ....

   ....

   ....

   Islam teaches that a criminal should be given the chance to reform, which can be achieved by imprisonment rather than corporal punishment.

   ....

   ....

   ....

   ....

   > This question asks you to consider two similar beliefs within a religious tradition (for example, within Christianity) or across two different religious traditions (such as Christianity and Islam). Two similar beliefs are given, from Christianity and Islam. Develop each belief fully by adding new information.

   (4 marks)

2. Explain **two** contrasting beliefs in contemporary British society about always being able to forgive others.

   In your answer you should refer to the main religious tradition of Great Britain and one or more other religious traditions.

   ....

   ....

   ....

   ....

   ....

   ....

   ....

   ....

   ....

   ....

   > This question asks you to consider two opposing beliefs. Remember that the main religious tradition of Great Britain is Christianity. You could choose to discuss two contrasting beliefs from within Christianity, or you could give contrasting beliefs from Christianity and Islam.

   (4 marks)

Had a go ☐ Nearly there ☐ Nailed it! ☐

Christianity Islam
Theme E
Components 2A and 2B

Religion, crime and punishment: Contrasting beliefs

1 Explain **two** similar religious beliefs about the use of the death penalty.

In your answer you must refer to one or more religious traditions.

> This question asks you to consider two similar beliefs within a religious tradition (for example, within Christianity) or across two different religious traditions (such as Christianity and Islam). Remember that Christians and Muslims have different views on whether the death penalty is acceptable. You need to identify two similar beliefs, so think carefully about which side of the argument you will choose to write your answer.

....
....
....
....
....
....
....
....
....

(4 marks)

2 Explain **two** contrasting beliefs in contemporary British society about the use of corporal punishment for criminals.

In your answer you should refer to the main religious tradition of Great Britain and one or more other religious traditions.

> This question asks you to consider two opposing beliefs about corporal (physical) punishment. Remember that the main religious tradition of Great Britain is Christianity. You could choose to discuss two contrasting beliefs from within Christianity, or you could give contrasting beliefs from Christianity and Islam.

....
....
....
....
....
....
....
....
....

(4 marks)

Christianity

Theme F

Components 2A and 2B

Had a go ☐   Nearly there ☐   Nailed it! ☐

Prejudice and discrimination

1 Which **one** of the following is **not** a type of discrimination?

Put a tick (✓) in the box next to the correct answer.

A Racism ☐
B Poverty ☐
C Ageism ☐
D Sexism ☐

> Look at the four options carefully. It is good revision practice to check your understanding of each term before deciding which one you think correctly answers the question. Note that this question asks you to identify the answer that is **not** a type of discrimination.

(1 mark)

Guided **2** Explain **two** religious beliefs about why discrimination is wrong.

Refer to sacred writings or another source of religious belief and teaching in your answer.

Many Christians believe discrimination is wrong because God created all humans equally. ....

> Two beliefs are given; you need to develop each one by adding further explanation and examples. Make sure you include a reference to a source of religious authority, such as the Bible or the Qur'an. You can do this either by quoting directly or summarising in your own words.

....

....

....

Some Christians believe discrimination is wrong because of Jesus' teachings in the Bible. ....

....

....

(5 marks)

116

Had a go ☐   Nearly there ☐   Nailed it! ☐

Islam

Theme F

Components 2A and 2B

Prejudice and discrimination

Guided 1 'Men and women should always be treated the same.'

Evaluate this statement.

In your answer you:

- should give reasoned arguments in support of this statement
- should give reasoned arguments to support a different point of view
- should refer to religious arguments
- may refer to non-religious arguments
- should reach a justified conclusion.

> Develop each view started here. Make sure you offer several views for and against the statement, with reference to Christian and Islamic beliefs and teachings, and non-religious arguments. End with a justified conclusion before checking your answer carefully for spelling, punctuation and grammar.

Some Muslims may agree with the statement as they believe Allah created all humans to be equal, although not the same. ....

....

....

....

Some non-religious believers may agree with the statement because they believe all humans are equal, although not for any religious reasons.

....

....

....

Some Christians may disagree with the statement because in some Christian denominations, such as Catholicism, women are not allowed to hold positions of authority. ....

....

....

....

In conclusion, ...

....

....

(12 marks + 3 SPaG marks)

Please complete your answer on your own paper if you need more space.

Christianity

Theme F

Components 2A and 2B

Had a go ☐ Nearly there ☐ Nailed it! ☐

Equality and freedom of religious belief

Guided

1 Give **two** reasons why religious believers support human rights.

1 Christians support human rights because they believe all life is sacred as God created it, therefore all humans deserve to be treated with respect through the recognition of human rights.

....

> One reason is given. Complete the answer by giving a second, different example – this could be from Christianity or Islam. Remember that you only need to state the reason; you don't need to explain it.

2 ....
....
....

(2 marks)

2 Explain **two** religious beliefs about equality.

Refer to sacred writings or another source of religious belief and teaching in your answer.

....
....
....
....

> Consider which two beliefs you could write about before you start your answer; you can include beliefs from Christianity or Islam. You need to refer to a source of religious authority, such as the Bible or the Qur'an, for at least one of the beliefs, by either quoting directly or summarising in your own words.

....
....
....
....
....
....
....
....
....

(5 marks)

Had a go ☐   Nearly there ☐   Nailed it! ☐

Islam

Theme F

Components 2A and 2B

Equality and freedom of religious belief

1. Which **one** of the following is the belief that every person is the same in terms of value and worth?

   Put a tick (✓) in the box next to the correct answer.

   A Sexism ☐
   B Equality ☐
   C Racism ☐
   D Tolerance ☐

   > Look at the four options carefully. It is good revision practice to check your understanding of each term before deciding which one you think correctly answers the question.

   (1 mark)

2. Explain **two** similar religious beliefs about the freedom of religion and belief.

   In your answer you must refer to one or more religious traditions.

   > This question asks you to consider two similar beliefs within a religious tradition (for example, within Christianity) or across two different religious traditions (such as Christianity and Islam). Develop each belief fully by giving additional information and examples.

   ....

   ....

   ....

   ....

   ....

   ....

   ....

   ....

   ....

   ....

   ....

   ....

   ....

   (4 marks)

Christianity — Theme F (Components 2A and 2B)

Had a go ☐   Nearly there ☐   Nailed it! ☐

Social justice

1 Which **one** of the following describes the idea of making sure there is equal distribution of wealth, opportunities and privileges in society?

Put a tick (✓) in the box next to the correct answer.

- A Fair pay ☐
- B Wealth ☐
- C Tolerance ☐
- D Social justice ✓

> Look at the four options carefully. It is good revision practice to check your understanding of each term before deciding which one you think correctly answers the question.

(1 mark)

2 Give **two** religious beliefs about social justice.

1 ....

2 ....

> You simply need to state two beliefs – you don't need to develop them. Think about what holy books teach about social justice or reasons why religious believers feel that fairness is important in the world.

(2 marks)

> Guided

3 Give **two** ways religious believers can work for social justice.

1 Christians can provide basic food supplies to those who are living in poverty, such as by donating to a food bank.

2 ....

> You simply need to state different ways that Christians or Muslims can help those who lack opportunities in society or who are living in poverty. Make sure they are different examples and focus specifically on what religious believers can do.

(2 marks)

Had a go ☐   Nearly there ☐   Nailed it! ☐

Islam — Theme F — Components 2A and 2B

Social justice

Guided 1 Give **two** reasons why social justice is important to religious believers.

1 Muslims feel social justice is important as Allah gave them the duty of helping others.

2 ....

....

> You simply need to state two reasons – you don't need to develop them. Make sure the reasons you give are different. One reason has been given here, so you need to add another one.

(2 marks)

2 'Religious believers should accept that there will always be inequality in the world.'

Evaluate this statement.

In your answer you:

- should give reasoned arguments in support of this statement
- should give reasoned arguments to support a different point of view
- should refer to religious arguments
- may refer to non-religious arguments
- should reach a justified conclusion.

> This type of question asks you to evaluate the given statement. Remember that some religious believers may agree with the statement and some may have alternative views. Think about the different reasons that may be offered to support each viewpoint, with reference to religious teachings and non-religious arguments. End with a justified conclusion before checking your answer carefully for spelling, punctuation and grammar.

....
....
....
....
....
....
....
....
....
....
....
....
....
....

(12 marks + 3 SPaG marks)

Please complete your answer on your own paper if you need more space.

Christianity — Theme F
Components 2A and 2B

Had a go ☐ Nearly there ☐ Nailed it! ☐

Responsibilities of wealth

Guided 1. Explain **two** similar religious beliefs about the duty of religious believers to help the poor.

In your answer you must refer to one or more religious traditions.

Christians believe they should follow the example of Jesus in caring for others and helping the poor.

> This question asks you to consider two similar beliefs within a religious tradition (for example, within Christianity) or across two different religious traditions (such as Christianity and Islam). Two similar beliefs are given; develop each one fully by adding new information or examples.

....
....
....
....

Muslims believe they have duties given to them by Allah, including the Pillar of Zakah.

....
....
....

(4 marks)

2. Explain **two** religious beliefs about the use of wealth.

Refer to sacred writings or another source of religious belief and teaching in your answer.

> Consider which two beliefs you could write about before you start your answer; you can include beliefs from Christianity or Islam. You also need to refer to a source of religious authority, such as the Bible or the Qur'an, for at least one of the beliefs, by either quoting directly or summarising in your own words.

....
....
....
....
....
....
....
....
....
....

(5 marks)

Had a go ☐   Nearly there ☐   Nailed it! ☐

Islam

Theme F

Components 2A and 2B

Responsibilities of wealth

1 'Every person has a responsibility to help those living in poverty.'

Evaluate this statement.

In your answer you:

- should give reasoned arguments in support of this statement
- should give reasoned arguments to support a different point of view
- should refer to religious arguments
- may refer to non-religious arguments
- should reach a justified conclusion.

> This type of question asks you to evaluate the given statement. Remember that some religious believers may agree with the statement and some may have alternative views. Think about the different reasons that may be offered to support each viewpoint, with reference to religious teachings and non-religious arguments. End with a justified conclusion before checking your answer carefully for spelling, punctuation and grammar.

....

....

....

....

....

....

....

....

....

....

....

....

....

....

....

....

....

(12 marks + 3 SPaG marks)

Please complete your answer on your own paper if you need more space.

Christianity — Theme F — Components 2A and 2B

Had a go ☐   Nearly there ☐   Nailed it! ☐

Exploitation of the poor

1 'It is wrong to lend money for profit.'

In your answer you:

- should give reasoned arguments in support of this statement
- should give reasoned arguments to support a different point of view
- should refer to religious arguments
- may refer to non-religious arguments
- should reach a justified conclusion.

> This type of question asks you to evaluate the given statement. Once you have considered arguments to support the statement, consider what alternative views you can give. You may include Christian, Islamic and non-religious views that argue the same point of view but for different reasons. Develop each reason fully and include religious teachings. End with a well-evaluated conclusion before checking your answer for spelling, punctuation and grammar.

....

....

....

....

....

....

....

....

....

....

....

....

....

....

....

....

....

....

....

....

(12 marks + 3 SPaG marks)

Please complete your answer on your own paper if you need more space.

Had a go ☐   Nearly there ☐   Nailed it! ☐

Islam — Theme F — Components 2A and 2B

Exploitation of the poor

Guided 1. Give **two** ways in which the poor in society may be exploited.

1 The poor may be paid unfairly for the work they complete. ....

2 ....

> Finish this answer by stating another way in which the poor are exploited. You don't need to develop the points, but make sure they are different.

(2 marks)

Guided 2. Explain **two** religious beliefs about why human trafficking is wrong.

Refer to sacred writings or another source of religious belief and teaching in your answer.

The Qur'an teaches that human trafficking is wrong because they accept the sanctity of life argument.

....

....

....

> Human trafficking is illegally moving people from one place to another, usually for forced labour or sexual exploitation. Two reasons why trafficking is wrong are identified in this guided answer. You need to develop each reason by adding further information and examples. Make sure you link at least one reason to a teaching from a source of religious authority, such as the Bible or the Qur'an.

the Qur'an teaches that human trafficking is wrong as Allah gave all humans the duty to care for and not harm each other. ....

....

....

....

....

....

(5 marks)

Christianity — Theme F
Components 2A and 2B

Had a go ☐ Nearly there ☐ Nailed it! ☐

Poverty and charity

1 Which **one** of the following is a term used to describe the situation when a person is lacking in the basics and struggles to live from day to day?

Put a tick (✓) in the box next to the correct answer.

- A Poverty ☐
- B Prejudice ☐
- C Social justice ☐
- D Wealth ☐

Check your understanding of what each term means before deciding which one is the correct answer.

(1 mark)

2 Give **two** examples of religious charities.

1 ....

2 ....

You could name one Christian charity and one Muslim charity, or two charities from the same religion.

(2 marks)

Guided

3 Explain **two** religious beliefs about charity.

Refer to sacred writings or another source of religious belief and teaching in your answer.

Christians believe it is important to show compassion towards others. Ephesians 4:32 teaches 'Be kind and compassionate to one another' and Jesus taught 'love your neighbour'. Christians believe they can do this by giving money to charity in order to help others. ....

The first part of the answer fully explains a Christian belief about charity and a teaching from the Bible supports this. You need to develop a second belief about charity, which could be from Christianity or Islam.

....

....

....

....

....

....

....

....

....

(5 marks)

Had a go ☐   Nearly there ☐   Nailed it! ☐

Islam — Theme F — Components 2A and 2B

Poverty and charity

Guided

1   Give **two** ways that those living in poverty can help themselves.

1   People in poverty can help themselves by actively looking for a job. ....

2   ....

....

....

You simply need to state two ways – you don't need to develop them. One example is given; you need to add a second one.

(2 marks)

2   Explain **two** religious beliefs about why religious believers should help those in poverty.

Refer to sacred writings or another source of religious belief and teaching in your answer.

....
....
....
....
....
....
....
....
....
....
....
....
....

Read this question carefully. It is asking you to explain why religious believers feel they should help those in poverty (not what they can do to help), so make sure you keep your answer focused on the question. You need to identify two beliefs and then develop each one by adding further information and examples. Make sure you link at least one belief to a teaching from a source of religious authority, such as the Bible or the Qur'an.

(5 marks)

Religion, human rights and social justice: Contrasting beliefs

Christianity / Islam — Theme F — Components 2A and 2B

Had a go ☐   Nearly there ☐   Nailed it! ☐

Guided

1 Explain **two** similar religious beliefs about the status of women in religion.

In your answer you must refer to one or more religious traditions.

Christians believe all humans – both men and women – are equal as God made all humanity.

....
....
....
....
....
....
....

> This question asks you to consider two similar beliefs within a religious tradition (for example, within Christianity) or across two different religious traditions (such as Christianity and Islam). One belief from Christianity is given; this needs to be developed. You then need to add a second similar religious belief – this can be from Christianity or Islam – and develop it fully.

(4 marks)

2 Explain **two** similar religious beliefs about how religious believers should use their wealth.

In your answer you must refer to one or more religious traditions.

....
....
....
....
....
....
....
....
....
....

> This question asks you to consider two similar beliefs within a religious tradition (for example, within Christianity) or across two different religious traditions (such as Christianity and Islam).

(4 marks)

128

Had a go ☐   Nearly there ☐   Nailed it! ☐

Christianity Islam
Theme F
Components 2A and 2B

Religion, human rights and social justice: Contrasting beliefs

Guided

1. Explain **two** contrasting beliefs in contemporary British society about how wealth should be used.

   In your answer you should refer to the main religious tradition of Great Britain and one or more other religious traditions.

   Christians believe wealth should be used in unselfish ways to help others. ....

   ....

   ....

   ....

   ....

   ....

   ....

   ....

   (4 marks)

   > This question asks you to consider two contrasting (opposing) beliefs. Remember that the main religious tradition of Great Britain is Christianity. You could choose to discuss beliefs from within Christianity, or from Christianity and Islam. Make sure you give specific examples in your development of each belief.

2. Explain **two** contrasting beliefs in contemporary British society about women being given positions of authority within religious life.

   In your answer you should refer to the main religious tradition of Great Britain and one or more other religious traditions.

   ....

   ....

   ....

   ....

   ....

   ....

   ....

   ....

   (4 marks)

   > This question asks you to consider two contrasting (opposing) beliefs. Remember that the main religious tradition of Great Britain is Christianity. You could choose to discuss beliefs from within Christianity, or from Christianity and Islam. Make sure the two ideas are different and develop each one fully.

Christianity — Theme G — Component 2B

Had a go ☐   Nearly there ☐   Nailed it! ☐

John's preparation for Jesus' ministry

1. Which **one** of the following describes the work completed by a religious leader?

   Put a tick (✓) in the box next to the correct answer.

   A Ministry   ☐
   B Education   ☐
   C Gospel   ☐
   D Messenger   ☐

   Check your understanding of each term before deciding which is the correct choice.

   (1 mark)

Guided

2. Explain **two** ways in which in which John is important for Christians today.

   You must refer to St Mark's Gospel in your answer.

   John is important to Christians today as St Mark's Gospel explains that he prepared the way for Jesus as the Messiah. ....

   Develop the point in this guided answer by adding more explanation. You then need to add a second point that is also fully developed. Remember to link at least one of your points to St Mark's Gospel.

   (5 marks)

Had a go ☐　Nearly there ☐　Nailed it! ☐

Christianity
Theme G
Component 2B

Jesus' baptism and temptation

1 Give **two** examples of events that happened at the baptism of Jesus.

   1 ....

   ....

   ....

   > You simply need to state two different events – you don't need to develop your answers further.

   2 ....

   ....

   (2 marks)

2 'The temptation of Jesus is less important than the baptism of Jesus.'

   Evaluate this statement.

   In your answer you:

   - should give reasoned arguments in support of this statement
   - should give reasoned arguments to support a different point of view
   - should refer to St Mark's Gospel
   - should reach a justified conclusion.

   > This question asks you to consider why some Christians may feel that Jesus' temptation holds more importance than his baptism, and to then consider possible reasons for alternative views. Remember that some Christians may feel both events have equal importance. Develop each reason fully and refer to St Mark's Gospel throughout. End with a well-evaluated conclusion before checking your answer for spelling, punctuation and grammar.

   ....
   ....
   ....
   ....
   ....
   ....
   ....
   ....
   ....
   ....
   ....
   ....
   ....

   (12 marks + 3 SPaG marks)

Please complete your answer on your own paper if you need more space.

Miracles of Jesus I

Christianity — Theme G — Component 2B

Had a go ☐ Nearly there ☐ Nailed it! ☐

1 Which **one** of the following is **not** a miracle performed by Jesus in St Mark's Gospel?

Put a tick (✓) in the box next to the correct answer.

- A The paralysed man ☐
- B Jairus' daughter ☐
- C Healing a man with a broken arm ☐
- D Feeding of the five thousand ☐

> Make sure you know the names of the miracles that Jesus performed and can identify them.

(1 mark)

Guided

2 'The miracles performed by Jesus prove that he was the Son of God.'

Evaluate this statement.

In your answer you:

- should give reasoned arguments in support of this statement
- should give reasoned arguments to support a different point of view
- should refer to St Mark's Gospel
- should reach a justified conclusion.

> Start by giving reasons that agree with the statement and then develop your reasons that disagree with it. Develop each reason fully and refer to St Mark's Gospel. End with a justified conclusion before checking for spelling, punctuation and grammar.

For many Christians, the miracles Jesus performed, such as healing the paralysed man, show that he was the Son of God, as normal humans cannot do what Jesus did. ....

....

....

....

....

However, some people may argue that, as the Bible was written so long ago and before modern scientific methods, some events that people could not explain may simply have been misinterpreted as 'miracles'.

....

....

....

....

....

(12 marks + 3 SPaG marks)

Please complete your answer on your own paper if you need more space.

Had a go ☐   Nearly there ☐   Nailed it! ☐

Christianity — Theme G — Component 2B

Miracles of Jesus II

Guided 1 Give **two** reasons why miracles are important for Christians today.

1 For many Christians, miracles prove the existence of God as they believe ordinary people cannot perform miracles. ....

2 ....
....
....

> State a second reason that is different from the first one given here. Think about what miracles may 'prove' about God for some Christians. Also consider how Christians today may view events described as miracles in the Bible.

(2 marks)

Guided 2 Explain **two** ways in which the story of the feeding of the five thousand is important for Christians today.

You must refer to St Mark's Gospel in your answer.

The feeding of the five thousand is important for Christians today as an example of the power of God through Jesus. Christians understand God to be omnipotent and, in this miracle in St Mark's Gospel, Jesus is seen to have this power as he ensures that every person in the crowd of five thousand is fed from five loaves and two fishes, which would normally be impossible. ....

....
....
....
....
....
....
....
....

> You will need to consider why miracles in general are important to Christians, but remember to focus your answer on the miracle of the feeding of the five thousand. Develop your answer by providing a detailed explanation of each way. Remember to refer to St Mark's Gospel throughout.

(5 marks)

Christianity — Theme G — Component 2B

Had a go ☐   Nearly there ☐   Nailed it! ☐

Caesarea Philippi and the transfiguration

Guided 1 Give **two** Christian beliefs about the conversation at Caesarea Philippi.

1 Christians believe the conversation at Caesarea Philippi was the first time the disciples accepted Jesus as the Messiah.

2 ....
....
....

> Jesus and his disciples had a conversation at Caesarea Philippi about who Jesus was and the events that would follow, including his death and resurrection. Complete this answer by giving a second belief about this event that is different from the first one. You simply need to state the belief – you don't need to explain it further.

(2 marks)

Guided 2 Explain **two** contrasting Christian understandings about the importance of the transfiguration of Jesus.

Some Christians view the transfiguration as a unique miracle, yet Jesus did not perform it.

....
....
....
....

> This question asks you two explain two contrasting understandings in depth. Think about why the transfiguration is important to Christians and what it may symbolise for them (a unique miracle; human meeting divine; Jesus as the Son of God; Jesus and his teaching as more important than Moses; ideas about eternal life). Complete this answer by developing each idea. For example, you could add more information or give examples.

Some Christians believe the transfiguration shows Jesus being recognised as the Son of God. ....
....
....
....
....
....
....
....

(4 marks)

Had a go ☐   Nearly there ☐   Nailed it! ☐

Christianity
Theme G
Component 2B

Passion prediction and James and John's request

Guided 1 'It was important that Jesus shared the passion prediction of his death with his disciples.'

Evaluate this statement.

In your answer you:

- should give reasoned arguments in support of this statement
- should give reasoned arguments to support a different point of view
- should refer to St Mark's Gospel
- should reach a justified conclusion.

> The passion prediction is where Jesus told his disciples what would happen to him in terms of his death. This would have shocked and scared the disciples, so include reasoned arguments to explain why it may have been important to share this information, as well as reasoned arguments to explain the drawbacks of doing so, referring to St Mark's Gospel throughout. Finish with a well-evaluated conclusion before checking for spelling, punctuation and grammar.

Jesus sharing the news of his death through the passion prediction would allow the disciples time to come to terms with the fact that he was going to die. He felt that understanding why he had to die as part of the prophecy would enable the disciples to accept his death more readily as having a higher purpose, which would support them in being able to continue his work in the world after his death.

....

(12 marks + 3 SPaG marks)

Please complete your answer on your own paper if you need more space.

Christianity — Theme G — Component 2B

Had a go ☐ **Nearly there** ☐ **Nailed it!** ☐

The story of Bartimaeus

Guided

1. Explain **two** contrasting understandings of the names given to Jesus in the story of Bartimaeus.

   In the story of Bartimaeus in St Mark's Gospel, Jesus is known as the Son of David. ....

   ....

   ....

   ....

   Jesus is also referred to in the story of Bartimaeus as a rabbi. ....

   ....

   ....

   ....

   Jesus is known by many names in St Mark's Gospel, many of which can be found in the story of Bartimaeus. Two contrasting examples are given. Complete the answer by explaining how Christians understand them.

   (4 marks)

2. Explain **two** ways in which the story of Bartimaeus is important for Christians today.

   You must refer to St Mark's Gospel in your answer.

   ....

   ....

   ....

   ....

   ....

   ....

   ....

   ....

   ....

   ....

   ....

   Jesus is referred to by many names in this story and it also shows that Bartimaeus had faith, which is why his sight was restored. You could use these ideas in your answer but make sure you develop each point fully.

   (5 marks)

Had a go ☐   Nearly there ☐   Nailed it! ☐

Christianity — Theme G — Component 2B

The entry into Jerusalem

1. Which **one** of the following describes how Jesus entered into Jerusalem at the beginning of the week before his crucifixion?

   Put a tick (✓) in the box next to the correct answer.

   A In secret at night ☐
   B As a 'king' with a big procession ☐
   C Afraid, as he knew he was going to be killed ☐
   D On the back of a donkey, happy and pleased to see people ☐

   > Look at the four options carefully before deciding which one you think correctly answers the question. To answer questions such as this, make sure you are familiar with the key events of St Mark's Gospel.

   (1 mark)

Guided

2. Explain **two** ways in which Jesus' entrance into Jerusalem is important for Christians today.

   You must refer to St Mark's Gospel in your answer.

   Jesus entered Jerusalem on a donkey. This is important for Christians today as it shows his humility and lack of self-importance. ....

   > Two different ideas about the way Jesus entered Jerusalem are outlined here. Develop each one by explaining fully why it holds importance for Christians today. Take care to refer to St Mark's Gospel throughout.

   ....
   ....
   ....
   ....
   ....

   Jesus was happy and cheerful as he entered Jerusalem. This is important for Christians today as it shows that, although his death was sad, it would fulfil the prophecy of Jesus saving humanity from sin. ....

   ....
   ....
   ....
   ....
   ....

   (5 marks)

Christianity
Theme G — Component 2B

Had a go ☐ Nearly there ☐ Nailed it! ☐

The Last Supper

1 Which **one** of the following is the truth that Jesus revealed at the Last Supper?

Put a tick (✓) in the box next to the correct answer.

- A One of the disciples would die with him ☐
- B One of the disciples would betray him ☐
- C One of the disciples would leave him ☐
- D One of the disciples would share the bread and wine with him ☐

> Look at the four options carefully before deciding which one you think correctly answers the question. To answer questions such as this, make sure you are familiar with the key events of St Mark's Gospel.

(1 mark)

Guided

2 Give **two** reasons why the Last Supper is important for Christians.

1 Christians believe Jesus gave important instructions at the Last Supper for how he should be remembered, which are part of the Eucharist service. ....

2 ....
....
....

> Complete this answer by giving another reason that is different from the first one. This question asks you about the importance of the Last Supper for Christians, so make sure each point is relevant to why Christians feel this event is important to them.

(2 marks)

3 Give **two** Christian beliefs about what happened at the Last Supper.

1 ....
....
....

2 ....
....

> You simply need to state two Christian beliefs about the events of the Last Supper – you don't need to explain them.

(2 marks)

Had a go ☐ Nearly there ☐ Nailed it! ☐

Christianity
Theme G
Component 2B

Jesus in Gethsemane and the trial

Guided 1 Give **two** Christian beliefs about the trial before the Jewish elders.

1 Christians believe the trial was illegal as people gave false testimony against Jesus. ....

2 ....

> State a second, different Christian belief about the trial before the Jewish elders. Remember that you don't need to explain the beliefs. The trial was not considered to be fair to Jesus – you could include this in your answer.

(2 marks)

Guided 2 Explain **two** ways in which the arrest and trials of Jesus are important for Christians. You must refer to St Mark's Gospel in your answer.

The arrest and trials of Jesus are important to Christians because they reflect the unfair way in which Jesus was treated and the injustice of this. For example, Jesus' trial in front of the Jewish elders was an illegal trial. St Mark's Gospel describes how people were brought into court to lie about Jesus and that, based on these lies, the authorities decided that Jesus was guilty of blasphemy.

> This guided answer explains one way in response to the question. Make sure you identify a second, different way and develop it by adding further information or detail. Remember also that you must refer to St Mark's Gospel, by either quoting directly or summarising in your own words.

(5 marks)

Christianity — Theme G — Component 2B

Had a go ☐   Nearly there ☐   Nailed it! ☐

The trial before Pilate, the crucifixion and burial

1 'The death of Jesus was Pilate's fault.'

Evaluate this statement.

In your answer you:

- should give reasoned arguments in support of this statement
- should give reasoned arguments to support a different point of view
- should refer to St Mark's Gospel
- should reach a justified conclusion.

> You need to consider all the people involved in Jesus being sentenced to death, including the Jewish authorities, the soldiers who arrested him and Pilate. You may also want to consider the disciples: Judas who betrayed him and Peter who denied him. Remember that Jesus knew he was going to die and it had been prophesied – this could mean that no one was to blame. Develop each argument fully and refer to St Mark's Gospel throughout. End with a well-evaluated conclusion before checking your answer for spelling, punctuation and grammar.

(12 marks + 3 SPaG marks)

Please complete your answer on your own paper if you need more space.

Had a go ☐ Nearly there ☐ Nailed it! ☐

Christianity
Theme G
Component 2B

The empty tomb

Guided

1. Explain **two** contrasting understandings of the resurrection of Jesus for Christians.

   Some Christians see Jesus' resurrection as evidence of a miracle that shows God's power and nature.

   ....

   This guided answer starts by identifying one way in which Christians might interpret and understand Jesus' resurrection. Complete the answer by developing the first point and adding another, contrasting understanding. Make sure you develop both ideas by giving further information or examples.

   (4 marks)

2. 'The resurrection of Jesus should convince everyone that God exists.'

   Evaluate this statement.

   In your answer you:
   - should give reasoned arguments in support of this statement
   - should give reasoned arguments to support a different point of view
   - should refer to St Mark's Gospel
   - should reach a justified conclusion.

   Try to include both Christian and contrasting non-religious arguments in your answer. End with a well-evaluated conclusion before checking your answer for spelling, punctuation and grammar.

   (12 marks + 3 SPaG marks)

Please complete your answer on your own paper if you need more space.

141

Christianity — Theme H — Component 2B

Had a go ☐   Nearly there ☐   Nailed it! ☐

The Kingdom of God I

1. Which **one** of the following is **not** an interpretation of the Kingdom of God?

   Put a tick (✓) in the box next to the correct answer.

   A Future hope ☐
   B Personal inner state ☐
   C House of God ☐
   D Present reality ☐

   > Remember that the Kingdom of God can be understood in different ways. You need to decide which answer is not one of those ways. Look at the four options carefully before making your final choice.

   (1 mark)

Guided

2. Explain **two** ways in which beliefs about the Kingdom of God are important for Christians.

   You must refer to St Mark's Gospel in your answer.

   Beliefs about the Kingdom of God help Christians to understand heaven. ....

   ....

   ....

   ....

   ....

   ....

   > This type of question asks you to give and then develop two different ideas by explaining them fully. Make clear links to what is said in St Mark's Gospel throughout your answer. This guided answer gives two ideas for you to develop further.

   Beliefs about the Kingdom of God help Christians to live in the way they believe God intends. ....

   ....

   ....

   ....

   ....

   ....

   ....

   ....

   (5 marks)

Had a go ☐ Nearly there ☐ Nailed it! ☐

Christianity

Theme H

Component 2B

The Kingdom of God II

1 Give **two** examples of teachings that Jesus used to help people understand the Kingdom of God.

   1 ....

   ....

   ....

   2 ....

   ....

   ....

> You simply need to state two different examples – you don't need to explain them in depth. Remember that Jesus' teachings included parables, which he used to help people understand complex ideas.

(2 marks)

2 'Jesus' teachings on the Kingdom of God are not relevant today.'

Evaluate this statement.

In your answer you:

- should give reasoned arguments in support of this statement
- should give reasoned arguments to support a different point of view
- should refer to St Mark's Gospel
- should reach a justified conclusion.

> Consider the arguments you could use to support this statement (non-religious believers may share this view) and then consider why Christians may argue against the statement. Develop each reason fully with reference to St Mark's Gospel. End with a well-evaluated conclusion before checking your answer for spelling, punctuation and grammar.

....

....

....

....

....

....

....

....

....

....

....

....

(12 marks + 3 SPaG marks)

Please complete your answer on your own paper if you need more space.

Christianity — Theme H — Component 2B

Had a go ☐ Nearly there ☐ Nailed it! ☐

Jesus' relationships: Women

1. Which **one** of the following did Jesus do to show he treated women as equal to men?

   Put a tick (✓) in the box next to the correct answer.

   A Jesus avoided speaking to women unless he knew them ☐
   B Jesus accepted women into his inner circle of trusted people ☐
   C Jesus allowed women to go to the Temple ☐
   D Jesus only allowed women to eat with him ☐

   > Look at the four options carefully before deciding which option is correct.

   (1 mark)

2. Explain **two** ways in which the way Jesus treated women is important for Christians today.

   You must refer to St Mark's Gospel in your answer.

   > You need to explain two different ways, developing each one fully. Remember to link to St Mark's Gospel in your answer. Note that this question asks you to focus on the importance for Christians **today**.

   ....

   (5 marks)

Had a go ☐ Nearly there ☐ Nailed it! ☐

Christianity

Theme H

Component 2B

Jesus' relationships: Gentiles and tax collectors

Guided

1 Give **two** reasons why Jesus' attitudes towards those disregarded in society are important to Christians today.

1 Jesus showed that it is wrong to discriminate against someone just because of who they are. This is important to Christians today as it reminds them of the importance of equality.

> A first reason is provided, which links to the importance for Christians today. To complete this answer, give a second, different reason, remembering to state the importance for Christians **today**.

2 ....

....

....

(2 marks)

2 Explain **two** ways in which Jesus' treatment of Gentiles and tax collectors is shown to be important in St Mark's Gospel.

You must refer to St Mark's Gospel in your answer.

> You need to explain two different ways, developing each one fully. Remember to link at least one of your ideas in this answer to St Mark's Gospel.

....

(5 marks)

145

Christianity — Theme H — Component 2B

Had a go ☐　Nearly there ☐　Nailed it! ☐

Jesus' relationships: The sick

Guided 1 Give **two** examples of Jesus' teachings from St Mark's Gospel about the importance of not treating those disregarded by society differently.

　　1　The story of the man with leprosy. ....

　　2　..

One of Jesus' teachings is correctly identified; you need to state a second teaching. Remember that you don't need to explain the points you make.

.... **(2 marks)**

Guided 2 Explain **two** ways in which Jesus' healing parables are important to Christians today.

You must refer to St Mark's Gospel in your answer.

Many Christians today believe the healing parables told by Jesus show the importance of people having faith. ....

Complete this guided answer. You need to explain two different ways in which Jesus' healing parables are important to Christians today, developing each way fully with clear links to St Mark's Gospel.

....

....

....

Many Christians today believe Jesus' healing parables show what God is like. ....

....

....

....

.... **(5 marks)**

Had a go ☐ Nearly there ☐ Nailed it! ☐

Christianity
Theme H
Component 2B

Faith and discipleship I

Guided

1 Explain **two** contrasting Christian beliefs about the disciples' mission to preach the gospel of Jesus after his death.

Some fundamental Christians believe the disciples were actually able to speak different languages, drive out demons and drink poison, as described in Mark 16. ....

....

....

....

.... **(4 marks)**

> You need to explain two contrasting ideas, developing each fully with information and examples. Develop the first idea and then add and develop a second, contrasting idea. Remember that there are different Christian understandings of the disciples' mission and what they were able to do.

2 'The disciples were given an impossible role to perform.'

Evaluate this statement.

In your answer you:

- should give reasoned arguments in support of this statement
- should give reasoned arguments to support a different point of view
- should refer to St Mark's Gospel
- should reach a justified conclusion.

> Consider the arguments to support this statement, as well as why some Christians may disagree with it (there are different Christian interpretations of the disciples' mission and their success). Develop each reason fully, with links to St Mark's Gospel. End with a well-evaluated conclusion before checking your answer for spelling, punctuation and grammar.

....

....

....

....

....

....

....

....

....

....

(12 marks + 3 SPaG marks)

Please complete your answer on your own paper if you need more space.

Christianity

Theme H — Component 2B

Had a go ☐ Nearly there ☐ Nailed it! ☐

Faith and discipleship II

1. Which **one** of the following is a prediction made by Jesus at the Last Supper?

   Put a tick (✓) in the box next to the correct answer.

   A All the disciples should be women ☐
   B The disciples would all gain eternal life in heaven ☐
   C Pilate would arrest Jesus ☐
   D The disciple Peter would deny knowing Jesus ☐

   > Look at the four options carefully before deciding which one you think correctly answers the question. To answer questions such as this, make sure you are familiar with the key events of St Mark's Gospel.

   (1 mark)

Guided

2. Explain **two** contrasting beliefs about the role of Jesus' disciples.

   Many Christians see the role of Jesus' disciples as a privileged one of great spiritual reward, despite the challenges they faced at the time.

   > Two beliefs are outlined in this guided answer. To complete the answer, develop both ideas fully.

   ....
   ....
   ....
   ....
   ....

   Other Christians may argue that the role of Jesus' disciples was extremely challenging. For example, ...

   ....
   ....
   ....
   ....

   (4 marks)

Answers

For questions marked * you will also be awarded up to 3 marks for accurate spelling and punctuation, the effective use of grammar to convey meaning and the use of a wide range of specialist terminology.

For many questions the answers may vary, but you could include some of the arguments and evidence given here.

CHRISTIANITY

Key beliefs

1. The nature of God I
1. D Inconsistent triad
2. For example:
   - Christians believe God is just and fair.
   - Christians believe God is omnipotent (all-powerful).
   - Christians believe God is all-loving.
   - Christians believe God controls everything.
3. For example:
   - The presence of evil and suffering challenges the nature of God, as if he were omnibenevolent (all-loving), he would want to stop his creation suffering.
   - The presence of evil and suffering challenges whether God is omnipotent (all-powerful), as if he were omnipotent he would have the power to stop evil and suffering.
   - The presence of evil and suffering challenges whether God is just, as if he were just he would not want people to suffer unfairly.
   - The presence of evil and suffering challenges whether God is omniscient (all-knowing), as if he were omniscient he would know how to prevent evil and suffering.
   - The presence of evil and suffering challenges whether God is fair, as if he were fair he would want to ensure all humans were treated fairly.

2. Evil and suffering
1. For example:
   - Christians could be inspired to try to help others who are suffering. They could do this through charity work. For example, Chad Varah established the Samaritans as a result of witnessing the suffering of others while he was working as a priest in London.
   - Christians may look to teachings from the Bible to help them cope with evil and suffering. For example, they may take comfort from Job's suffering and see their own suffering as a similar test of faith.
   - Christians may spend more time in prayer. They may ask God for the strength to cope with suffering, for themselves and for others. They may believe God hears and will answer their prayers.
2. For example:
   - Many Christians believe there is a purpose to evil and suffering: Psalm 119:66–67 offers reassurance that evil and suffering give people the opportunity to follow the example set by Jesus so that humans can live as God intended.
   - Some Christians believe evil and suffering may be a test of faith. They may look to the example of Job in the Bible (Job 1:22). He endured much suffering yet did not lose his faith as he believed suffering was part of God's plan for him.
   - Christians believe evil and suffering gives them the opportunity to help others: they could help reduce the suffering of others through charities such as the Samaritans. Ephesians 4:32 states that people have a duty to be compassionate towards each other.

3. The nature of God II
1.* Arguments in support:
   - The Trinity helps Christians to understand the three distinct aspects of God: God as Father, Son and Holy Spirit. The Trinity reinforces the idea of Christianity as a monotheistic religion: that although God can be understood in three ways, there is still only one God. Passages in the Bible such as Genesis 1:1, Mark 1:9 and Matthew 28:19 help Christians understand that God is Father, Son and Holy Spirit, and this is also declared in the Nicene Creed.

   Arguments in support of other views:
   - Some Christians may find the idea of the Trinity (one God but three parts) confusing and contradictory. This could mean that they struggle to gain a clear understanding of God.
   - Some Christians may prefer to understand what God is like through words that describe his nature, such as omnipotent or all-loving.
   - Some people, especially non-religious believers, may misunderstand the idea of the Trinity as meaning that Christians believe in three different Gods.

4. Creation
1. A Genesis
2. For example:
   - The Bible teaches that the universe was created at a command from God: John 1:1 says 'In the beginning was the Word, and the Word was with God and the Word was God.' This suggests that God used his power to create the universe from one command.
   - The Bible teaches that God created everything from nothing: Genesis 1:1–2 speaks of the Earth being 'formless and empty' before describing how God created the universe and everything within it.
   - The Bible teaches that God created the world in six days: this can be interpreted literally by some Christians as six 24-hour days, whereas other Christians interpret it symbolically as referring to six periods of time. Genesis 1 details how God created something different on each 'day', for example, creating light and darkness on the first day.

5. The afterlife
1. For example:
   - For many Christians, belief in the afterlife is important because it answers the question of what happens after death.
   - For many Christians, belief in the afterlife is important because it gives life meaning and purpose.
   - For many Christians, belief in the afterlife is important because it is supported by the resurrection of Jesus.
   - For many Christians, belief in the afterlife is important because it means Christians try to understand how God wants them to behave to achieve eternal life.
2. For example:
   - A belief in the afterlife will influence Christians to live good lives so that they can be rewarded in heaven and avoid going to hell. This is in accordance with God's rules. A belief in the afterlife will influence Christians to follow Jesus' teachings and example so that they can achieve eternal life after death. For example, Jesus taught 'treat others as you want to be treated' and 'love thy neighbour'.
   - A belief in the afterlife will encourage Christians to pray to God regularly to ask for forgiveness as they believe God will forgive their sins so they can go to heaven.

Jesus Christ and salvation

6. Jesus as the Son of God
1. For example:
   - Jesus was both human and divine.
   - Jesus fulfilled the prophecy of Christ coming to Earth as the Saviour who was promised by God.
   - Jesus was able to perform miracles.
   - Jesus was resurrected after death.
   - Jesus was born to a human mother.
2. For example:
   - Christians try to follow the example and teachings of Jesus in their lives, as they believe he came to Earth to show them how they should behave.
   - Christians feel the incarnation proves that Jesus was the Son of God. This helps them understand God's omnipotence and love for them by coming to Earth in human form.

- Christians use Jesus' incarnation to reinforce other key Christian beliefs. For example, Jesus' resurrection provides evidence of an afterlife.

7. Crucifixion, resurrection and ascension

1* Arguments in support:
- Some Christians may agree with the statement, as the resurrection of Jesus is one of the key beliefs held in Christianity. Jesus came to Earth with the purpose of saving the sins of the whole world and repairing the relationship between God and humanity. The resurrection is evidence that Jesus was the Son of God.
- Some Christians may see the resurrection as more important than the crucifixion because through the resurrection Jesus is seen to have conquered death. Christians believe the resurrection means they do not need to fear death. This is supported by John 11:25, where Jesus states that if Christians follow him they will have eternal life.
- Jesus rising from the dead and then ascending to heaven is seen as evidence for an afterlife. All Christians hold this belief to be evidence of life after death and the existence of heaven.

Arguments in support of other views:
- Some Christians may argue that the crucifixion is more important than the resurrection as it helped restore the relationship between God and humanity. Jesus died on the cross in order to atone for the sins of humanity. Without this important event, Christianity would not exist.
- Some Christians may argue that the events of the crucifixion and resurrection are both important, but it is the ideas of salvation and atonement that are most important, not just the events.

8 Salvation and atonement

1 C Atonement
2 For example:
- Christianity teaches that God sent Jesus to Earth in human form so that humanity could achieve salvation. John 3:16 states that God loves the world, which is why he sent Jesus, and that anyone who believes in Jesus will achieve eternal life.
- Christianity teaches that the sins of humanity are forgiven through God sending Jesus to Earth: Acts 4:11–12 teaches that Jesus was perfect and without sin, so he offered salvation for humans through his sacrifice. Christianity teaches that salvation was needed due to the breakdown of the relationship between God and humanity, which occurred when Adam and Eve disobeyed God in the Garden of Eden. Acts 4:11–12 says that salvation was only found through Jesus.

Worship and festivals

9. Forms of worship

1 C Liturgical
2 For example:
- Some Christians choose to worship God using liturgical worship, which is where Christians worship together following a set pattern and structure. This could involve attending a service of Mass/Eucharist/Holy Communion on a Sunday, where bread and wine (symbolising the body and blood of Jesus) are given to the congregation. The Book of Common Prayer states that it is a Christian duty to worship God.
- Some Christians may choose to worship God privately and alone. This can take the form of praying, reading the Bible or retreating and spending time alone. John 4:23 describes how God is looking for those who worship him in the right way.
- Some Christians prefer to worship God spontaneously and not follow a set pattern. This is known as non-liturgical worship. They may choose to worship through clapping, singing, dancing or even speaking in tongues. Psalm 95:6 says 'Come let us bow down in worship'. Some Christians may interpret this as meaning that worship can take any form they prefer.

10. Prayer

1 For example:
- Christians pray to God to get closer to and communicate with him.
- Christians pray to God to praise him.
- Christians pray to God to thank him.
- Christians pray to God to ask for his help.
- Christians pray to God to say sorry.

2 For example:
- Christians may choose to use set prayers that are found in their prayer book and used in Sunday services of worship when they pray as a group with others. Many set prayers reflect key Christian beliefs and may praise or thank God for what he has done and provided.
- Christians may choose to speak aloud the Lord's Prayer, which is one of the most famous prayers because Jesus taught it to his followers. It contains many key beliefs in Christianity, such as ideas of forgiveness.
- Christians may choose informal prayers, where they speak their own words directly to God, perhaps individually and privately. Some Christians may believe this type of prayer helps them to connect to God personally and ask individually for help in their lives.

11. Baptism

1 B Sacrament
2 For example:
- Most Christians have an infant baptism ceremony to welcome a baby into the Christian faith. Parents and godparents make promises on behalf of the child, the vicar or priest makes the sign of the cross on the baby's forehead and water is poured onto their head from the font. A lighted candle is given to represent the light of Jesus.
- Some Christians do not support infant baptism as they feel that children are not old enough to make the decision for themselves; they prefer to baptise adults only. They may choose to have a child dedication ceremony instead of a baptism, where the child is officially named and introduced to the Christian congregation.
- Some Christians practise adult or believer's baptism, where the person makes the choice for themselves to enter the Christian faith. Each individual is asked questions about their faith and makes a personal testimony about why they wish to become a Christian. They are baptised through full immersion in a baptistery pool.

12. Eucharist

1 Arguments in support:
- Some Christians may argue that prayer – especially informal, private prayer when a Christian prays individually to God – may help to develop a more personal relationship with God. Although they may recognise that celebrating the Eucharist with other Christians is one method of praising God, they may feel that a more individual connection can be developed through individual prayer.
- Some Christians may feel that through individual prayer they can reflect and ask God for help in their lives, praise him and offer him thanks, and ask for forgiveness when they have done wrong. Some Christians may argue that as everyone is judged individually after death, the individual relationship with God is of more importance than a sacrament. Each Christian can develop their relationship with God through individual prayer.

Arguments in support of other views:
- Some Christians may argue that celebrating the Eucharist is more important than praying individually to God as it is one of the most important sacraments in Christianity and all Christian denominations recognise it in some form. It recalls the Last Supper, when Jesus gave instructions to the disciples to remember him through taking the bread and wine. It also recalls Jesus' sacrifice through which the sins of humanity were forgiven and gives Christians the opportunity to praise God as a community.
- Some Christians may argue that group prayer, such as that during the Eucharist service, is more powerful, and therefore more important, than individual prayer. The Eucharist is

a regular sacrament that brings the Christian community together and shows that they are united by shared beliefs in the power of the sacrament ceremony.

13. Pilgrimage

1 Arguments in support:
- Some Christians may argue that, as a practice, pilgrimage has little value. Other practices such as helping in the local community or charity work can have positive outcomes for many people and so may be seen to have more benefit.
- Some Christians may believe, as there is no requirement to complete a pilgrimage in Christianity (as there is in some other religions), it does not hold as much importance. Although there are references to pilgrimage in the Bible (for example, Luke 2:41–42), there is no direct rule for Christians to complete a pilgrimage.
- Many Christians believe faith is personal and can be expressed in ways other than pilgrimage. They may respect that, for some, pilgrimage is a way to celebrate their faith, but may see regular worship and prayer, giving to charity or taking part in church activities as more important.

Arguments in support of other views:
- Some Christians may believe places of pilgrimage hold great significance within the faith and that visiting them helps them to develop their understanding of Christianity and their relationship with God. For example, Christian pilgrims may go to Lourdes to see where Bernadette had her experience and take of the healing waters there. Some Christians may argue that pilgrimage has more importance today than ever: as life is so busy, going on a pilgrimage creates time and opportunity for them to reflect on their faith. Pilgrimage is also an opportunity for them to meet and share experiences with other Christians on pilgrimage.
- Some Christians may argue that the stories and events behind Christian spiritual places should be celebrated. Many Christians visit places such as Bethlehem and Jerusalem to trace the history of the religion; Lourdes, where the Virgin Mary was seen; and Iona, where saints lived and their prayers were answered. These experiences can help Christians to deepen their sense of being part of a worldwide Christian community, as well as their faith in God.

14. Celebrations

1 For example:
- Christians celebrate Christmas by singing carols.
- Christians celebrate Christmas by going to Midnight Mass services.
- Christians celebrate Christmas by putting on nativity plays.
- Christians celebrate Christmas by taking part in special Christmas Day services.
- Christians celebrate Christmas by giving and receiving religious charity cards.

2 For example:
- Christians attend special services at Easter to mark the death of Jesus on the cross. There may be a re-enactment of the events of the crucifixion, perhaps with Jesus carrying his cross and being crucified on Good Friday. Christians may think about Jesus' sacrifice and celebrate his resurrection, which reflects key Christian beliefs (as stated in the Bible) in eternal life, God's love for the world in sending Jesus and following Jesus leading to eternal life.
- Christians may come together as a family during the Easter weekend to remember the sacrifice of Jesus and his resurrection. They may attend an Easter service in church and have a special meal at home. Hot cross buns may be eaten to remind people of Jesus' death on the cross. Christians may spend time in prayer and reflect on teachings such as John 11:25, which reminds them of the importance of believing in Jesus so they can follow his example and achieve eternal life after death.
- Some Christians send Easter cards and give presents on Easter Sunday to remember Jesus' sacrifice and the joy at his overcoming death through the resurrection (often represented by giving hollow chocolate Easter eggs). Sharing teachings from the Bible, such as 1 Corinthians 15:12, reinforces the message that Jesus was resurrected after death and of eternal life.

The role of the Church

15. The church in the local community

1 Arguments in support:
- There are many key Christian teachings about helping others, such as 'Love your neighbour as yourself' (Matthew 22:39) and the Parable of the Sheep and the Goats (Matthew 25). Many Christians believe that by working with other church members they can provide help in the local community, such as by running food banks to support the most vulnerable during times of crisis.
- Many Christians believe the church is more than just a building: it represents a group of people with shared beliefs and interests and so it is the best place from which to offer help to others in the local community. For example, people from local churches may go out into the community as outreach workers. Many Christians believe the local church, and especially the vicar, plays an invaluable role in supporting those in the local community, such as by educating them, bringing them together and helping them in times of need.

Arguments in support of other views:
- Some Christians may argue that the most important function of a church is to bring people together in the Christian faith, providing a spiritual centre of faith and sanctuary. Although this can happen by helping those in the local community, it is not the most important role.
- Many Christians accept that the church has many functions. However, they may argue that its primary function is as a place of worship and prayer. Some Christians may believe the most important role of the local church is the celebration of religious milestones such as religious festivals (Christmas and Easter) and rites of passage (marriage and death).

16. Sharing faith

1 For example:
- Christian churches can help Church growth by going out to places as a missionary.
- Christian churches can help Church growth by education programmes such as the Alpha course.
- Christian churches can help Church growth by televangelism.
- Christian churches can help Church growth through community projects.
- Christian churches can help Church growth by holding faith conferences.

2 For example:
- One way the Church supports the growth of Christianity is by organising education classes where those who are not part of the Christian faith can learn more about the Christian religion and engage in debate and discussions about the faith. These courses are known as Alpha courses and they are run in local communities. They encourage people who are not members of the Church community to find out more so they can join the Christian faith.
- Community projects, such as providing a play area for children in the local community or providing an allotment for people to use, can bring people in the local community together, helping to draw non-Christians into the Church community.
- The Church could make use of televangelism. Religious channels such as God TV organise Christian programmes such as discussion forums, concerts and conferences. These are televised to reach a wider range of people and share the messages of Christianity.

17. Importance of the worldwide Church I

1 Arguments in support:
- Christianity teaches that all Christians have a duty to help others, including when people are persecuted. The Bible teaches 'Love one another' (John 13:34) and 'Love your enemies and

pray for those who persecute you' (Matthew 5:44). Many Christians believe putting these teachings into action is what God wants and so they have a responsibility to act when others are persecuted. They may refer to Christian individuals and organisations, such as the Barnabas Fund and Christian Aid, which act to support those who are persecuted as well as challenge persecution. Christians believe churches have a duty from God to bring reconciliation to communities by educating people and making them aware of persecution. This view is supported by Christian teachings on forgiveness, such as Mark 11:25, which says that if you expect forgiveness from God you should be willing to forgive others. Faith leaders may therefore try to bring people from different faiths together within the local community so that they can better understand each other and learn to work together rather than be in conflict.
- The Bible teaches that God is just and therefore many Christians believe they should act justly in the world. This includes putting pressure on those in authority, such as governments, to act to bring an end to persecution in the world.

Arguments in support of other views:
- Some Christians may argue that, although they can respond to persecution they witness personally, they have little power individually to respond to persecution in society in general or in other countries. This is the responsibility of those in authority. Some Christians may be concerned that often persecution happens in areas of conflict in the world and that therefore they may make a troubled situation worse or get hurt if they intervene. Although there are many teachings on helping others in the Bible, there are also teachings on the sanctity of life.
- Some Christians may argue that they have a greater responsibility to look after their loved ones than intervene in risky situations they know little about.

18. Importance of the worldwide Church II

1 D Muslim Aid
2 For example:
   - An organisation such as CAFOD works to provide food, water and shelter in times of emergency and crisis in the world for those facing poverty. They may do this after a natural disaster when people have lost their belongings or in times of conflict, such as when people have had to leave their country and become refugees.
   - Christian Aid is a charity that works across Africa and Asia to provide medical care and aid where people cannot afford it. For example, it has provided medical care in poorer countries where the spread of HIV/AIDS is rapid and medical programmes are not established to support those who are infected. Tearfund supports groups in their communities, especially focusing on vulnerable and disadvantaged people living in poverty. It has spoken out against exploitation in places such as Nepal, where people are not given their human rights or equality in terms of work, money or standard of living. Tearfund believes it has a duty from God to help those in poverty.

ISLAM
Key beliefs
19. The six articles of faith in Sunni Islam

1 For example:
   - Muslims recite belief in the Oneness of Allah.
   - Muslims may read the Qur'an daily.
   - Muslims may be aware that Allah is watching constantly.
   - Muslims may try to live as God wants in order to go to heaven after death.
   - Muslims may try to follow Muhammad's example.
2* Arguments in support:
   - Some Muslims would agree with the statement because there are many similarities between the six articles of faith and the five roots of Usul ad-Din, including belief in Tawhid and prophethood. Also, any differences between Sunni and Shi'a Muslims are minimal and come mostly from issues of authority and leadership; the essential beliefs are the same.
   - Although some of the beliefs in the six articles of faith and the five roots of Usul ad-Din are named differently, they are based on the same ideas. For example, the six articles of faith include teachings about life after death and the five roots of Usul ad-Din refer to a Day of Judgement and the resurrection.

Arguments in support of other views:
   - Some Muslims would disagree with the statement because most Sunni Muslims and Shi'a Muslims do not see their beliefs as the same. They may refer to the key differences between the six articles of faith and the five roots of Usul ad-Din. For example, Shi'a Muslims place greater emphasis on Allah being fair and just, yet this idea is not made explicit in the six articles. Also, Sunni Muslims include the Qur'an and other holy books in the six articles and Shi'a Muslims do not include these in their five roots. Similarly, Shi'a Muslims recognise the successors of Muhammad as part of the five roots of Usul ad-Din.

20. The five roots of Usul ad-Din in Shi'a Islam

1 For example:
   - One of the five roots is Tawhid (belief in the Oneness of Allah).
   - One of the five roots is Adalat (belief in divine justice).
   - One of the five roots is Nubuwwah (belief in prophethood).
   - One of the five roots is Imamate (belief in successors to Muhammad).
   - One of the five roots is Mi'ad (belief in the Day of Judgement and the resurrection).
2 For example:
   - One of the five roots is about the Day of Judgement, so Shi'a Muslims may live with the awareness that Allah will judge them after death. This may mean that they try to live according to the rules set down by Allah, for example by following the Five Pillars of Islam.
   - One of the five roots is about prophethood, so Shi'a Muslims may follow the messages given to prophets as they believe them to be directly from Allah. For example, Muslims may believe the messages of the Qur'an given to Muhammad will help guide them in their lives.
   - One of the five roots is Tawhid, which is belief in the Oneness of Allah. Muslims may follow this through submitting to Allah in every act they perform.

21. The Oneness and nature of God

1* Arguments in support:
   - Many Muslims would agree with the statement as Tawhid is the fundamental belief in Islam, describing the idea that Muslims accept only one God and are monotheistic. As all other beliefs in Islam relate to the idea of Tawhid (the six articles of faith for Sunni Muslims, the five roots of Usul ad-Din for Shi'a Muslims, the Shahadah), it is the best way for Muslims to understand and relate to Allah.
   - Tawhid describes the unity of Allah, seen in Surah 112: 'He is Allah, who is One'. This describes the essential nature of God as being One, having no start or end. Allah is unique as nothing is equal to him.

Arguments in support of other views:
   - Although Muslims view Tawhid as central to understanding Allah, other terms and methods can be used. For example, Muslims believe Allah is transcendent, meaning he is beyond human understanding, as well as immanent (close and acting within the world). This demonstrates Allah's powerful nature yet is a little contradictory for some people as he is seen as being both beyond human understanding but also close to and acting within the world.
   - Some Muslims may find the concept of Tawhid difficult to understand.

They may believe the 99 names of Allah, which describe the many aspects of his nature, may be easier to focus on in order to understand him.
- Although some Muslims see Tawhid as an important central belief, they may believe other ideas should be used alongside it in order to better understand Allah and relate to him. These include ideas of Allah as a creator and judge, omnibenevolent and merciful.

22. Angels
1   A Jibril
2   For example:
- Angels are important in Islam as they are messengers between Allah and humans. For example, Muhammad received the Qur'an from the angel Jibril and, without this important message, Muslims today would not have the guidance of the words of Allah. The Qur'an teaches that Jibril appeared to Muhammad over 23 years and taught him the words of the Qur'an.
- Allah gives some angels important roles. Muslims believe Izra'il will blow a trumpet to signal the coming of the Day of Judgement. Teachings such as Surah 32:11 remind Muslims to live their lives according to Allah's intentions, as they will be judged.
- Some angels are reminders to Muslims of key beliefs in Islam. For example, Mika'il is the Angel of Mercy who is believed to reward those who deserve it in the afterlife, reminding Muslims to live their lives as Allah intended.

23. al-Qadr and Akhirah
1* Arguments in support:
- Some Muslims would agree with the statement as the Qur'an is descriptive about the nature of hell as a punishment for those who deserve it. For example, Surah 3:131 describes hell as a place of pain and torment for unbelievers. It can therefore be argued that Muslims should fear the Day of Judgement and aim to live as Allah intended by following his rules.
- Many Muslims may fear the Day of Judgement (Surah 17:71), when Muslims believe Allah will judge them fairly for the way they have lived, if they have not always led a good life. Islam teaches that Allah gave humans free will, although he already knows what they will do. Muslims are taught to understand that abusing their free will has consequences, one of which is they will be judged on their actions in the afterlife.

Arguments in support of other views:
- Some Muslims may disagree. They may believe death is not the end and they should look forward to life continuing. They may believe if they have lived their life according to the Qur'an and the example set by Muhammad, they have nothing to fear from Allah's judgement. This view is promoted in Surah 17:71, which describes the books of the deeds of Muslims that are used to decide their fate.
- Islam teaches that Allah is merciful. This is shown in the Qur'an (Surah 76:30) when it talks of Allah's mercy. Muslims believe if they are sorry for the things they have done wrong, Allah will treat them fairly.
- Muslims believe Allah created the universe for humanity and so they should make the most of the gift of life from Allah, rather than living in fear of the Day of Judgement.

Authority
24. Risalah (prophethood)
1   C Ibrahim
2   For example:
- Islam teaches that there have been many prophets; the Qur'an names 25 different ones. Some of these include Abraham, Ishmael and Jesus, who are described in Surah 2:136 as revealing messages from Allah.
- Islam teaches that some prophets are given special importance as they wrote down messages directly from Allah. Prophets who have a written message are called rasuls and they include Muhammad, who was given the Qur'an, the final unaltered message from Allah. Surah 53:4–5 teaches that the Qur'an is Allah's 'revelation revealed' that he shared with Muhammad.
- Islam teaches that Muhammad is a particularly important prophet as he was the final prophet and no more will come after him. Muslims refer to Muhammad as 'the Seal of the Prophets' as he brought the final unaltered message from Allah to humanity. In his final sermon, Muhammad made this clear by stating that 'no prophet or messenger will come after me'.

25. The holy books
1   For example:
- Muslims read passages from the Qur'an in the Jummah service in the mosque.
- Muslims read the words of the Qur'an daily in their worship.
- Muslims include passages from the Qur'an in marriage ceremonies.
- Many Muslims turn to the Qur'an when they need advice or guidance in their lives.
- Many Muslims look to the Qur'an as a source of law in family or business matters.
2   For example:
- Muslims often read the Qur'an when they need support or guidance in their lives. They believe it is the final message given to Muhammad from Allah, so they respect it. They may believe teachings from the Qur'an can help them to make decisions that please Allah so they will be rewarded in the afterlife.
- Many Muslims choose to learn the Qur'an by heart, as Muhammad did, to maintain the true meaning of its words. Muslims believe the Qur'an was passed to Muhammad in oral form as he was illiterate. Muslims feel it is important to learn the Qur'an in its original language of Arabic to enable them to obtain its correct meaning.
- Many Muslims use the Qur'an both in their daily lives and within worship. Muslims recite the words of the Qur'an in prayer and words are spoken from it in the Jummah service held each Friday in the mosque. Muslims believe the Qur'an is an important source of authority in Islam as it comes directly from Allah.

26. The Imamate in Shi'a Islam
1* Arguments in support:
- Some Shi'a Muslims may accept the statement as they accept the Imamate as part of their beliefs. They believe after the death of Muhammad 12 imams succeeded him to lead other Muslims. Shi'a Muslims believe imams have the same characteristics as prophets and that Allah divinely appointed them to lead others in the Islamic faith.
- Shi'a Muslims believe imams are infallible humans who rule over the ummah. They are seen as an important source of authority in interpreting Islamic law and guiding Muslims. Muslims believe after the death of Muhammad Allah did not abandon them. The imams are his way of giving them a further source of authority and guidance.
- The imamate is an important source of authority in Islam. It is recognised as one of the five roots of Usul ad-Din, the basic foundations and beliefs of Shi'a Islam.

Arguments in support of other views:
- Sunni Muslims may disagree. They recognise that the imam has a role in Islam but they place less emphasis on the authority of the imam than Shi'a Muslims do because they see the role of the imam as being more local in the mosque. They do not believe imams are divinely appointed by Allah; rather, they believe they are simply selected from within a local community to lead prayers in the mosque and offer guidance to Muslims who may need it.
- Some Muslims may recognise the imam as holding some importance as a source of authority within Islam, but they may view other sources of authority, such as the Qur'an, which provides the direct revelation of Allah, and the Hadith and Sunnah, which are the actions and words of Prophet Muhammad, as higher sources.

153

Worship

27. The Five Pillars and the Ten Obligatory Acts

1 Arguments in support:
- The Five Pillars are the basic duties that all Muslims have to perform. For example, the first Pillar (the Shahadah) sums up what it means to be a Muslim and demonstrates a Muslim's commitment to their faith; the second Pillar (Salah) is praying five times a day, which is regular communication with Allah. The Five Pillars are seen to uphold and support the religion, providing a solid foundation of practices on which all Islamic beliefs are based.
- Many Muslims understand Islam as being about submission to Allah. For many Muslims, when they perform the Five Pillars they believe they are following Islam as Allah intended.

Arguments in support of other views:
- Some Muslims would argue that the 'basis' of the Islamic faith is the key belief of 'submission to Allah'. Although this is achieved through key ideas such as the Five Pillars, many Muslims may not class them as the 'basis' of the faith.
- The Ten Obligatory Acts are more important to Shi'a Muslims (although four of the Five Pillars of Islam are included in the Ten Obligatory Acts). Therefore, they would be likely to support a different view. They may believe that although the Five Pillars are important and do form part of the basis of the religion, other beliefs such as jihad, khums and the other acts identified in the Ten Obligatory Acts are equally important.
- Some Muslims may argue that the only key idea at the basis of Islam is Allah (Tawhid). Although acceptance of this belief is seen within the Five Pillars, some Muslims may argue that it is this belief alone that is central to the Islamic faith.

28. The Shahadah

1 For example:
- Muslims whisper the words of the Shahadah into the ears of newborn babies.
- Muslims recite the Shahadah before death.
- Muslims recite the Shahadah out loud in front of witnesses.
- Muslims recite the Shahadah throughout the day.
- Muslims recite the Shahadah as part of Salah (compulsory prayer).

2 For example:
- Sunni Muslims accept the Shahadah as the first of the Five Pillars of Islam and the declaration of faith. It includes two beliefs: there is no God but Allah and Muhammad is the Prophet of Allah.
- Shi'a Muslims do not recognise the Shahadah as a separate Pillar. However, they do accept it as one of the Ten Obligatory Acts. Shi'a Muslims add a third belief to the beliefs in One God (Allah) and in Muhammad as his messenger, which is that 'Ali is the protector of Allah'.

29. Salah I

1 **D** Jummah
2 For example:
- Salah is regular communication with Allah.
- Salah is required to develop a personal relationship with Allah.
- Salah is the second of the Five Pillars of Islam.
- Salah is a duty and compulsory in Islam.
- Muhammad established Salah.

3 For example:
- Muslims are expected through Salah to worship Allah and recognise his power. For example, Islam teaches that prayer verses should be read from the Qur'an when Salah is performed. This can be done through reciting passages such as Surah 1, which talks of the power of Allah and his characteristics.
- Islam teaches that men should attend the mosque to pray but women do not have to. This is because men and women are seen to have different roles in Islam, with men being the providers and protectors and women being responsible for looking after the house and children. Men are given the key responsibilities of teaching the Islamic faith to children and attending the mosque to pray.
- Islam teaches that Salah can happen anywhere as long as it is clean. Muslims are expected to pray regularly to develop a relationship with Allah and the Qur'an teaches that as long as wudu has been performed and prayer is completed in a clean place, this is acceptable.

30. Salah II

1 Arguments in support:
- Some Shi'a Muslims may agree with the statement because they combine their prayers into three daily prayers rather than five, so although they still follow Salah as a duty, they may agree that they should not have to pray five times a day. They may agree that Muslims should have the freedom to pray when they choose. Some Muslims believe Salah is the minimum number of times prayer should take place each day and so might argue that they can always choose to perform extra prayers, known as du'ah, outside of Salah. Some Muslims might argue that praying at set times can be difficult to achieve for a person with a job and so, if a Muslim wants to pray, they should be free to do so whenever they choose.

Arguments in support of other views:
- Most Muslims would disagree, as they believe Salah is a duty from Allah that has to be performed. Regular prayer is compulsory in Islam and not a choice. Sunni Muslims believe prayer should be completed as Allah intended. Shi'a Muslims may combine some prayers, yet they still believe prayer is an important duty that should happen at prescribed times.
- Some Sunni Muslims believe a Muslim who does not pray five times a day is an 'unbeliever'. As Islam teaches that those who believe in Allah will be rewarded in heaven after death, they may argue that praying fewer than the five set times is wrong and will go against them when judged by Allah after death.

Duties and festivals

31. Sawm

1 Arguments in support:
- Some Muslims may agree with the statement. They may argue that the supposed benefits of fasting (for example, getting closer to Allah) could be achieved through other means. For example, giving charity through the Pillar of Zakah has more impact towards others than fasting and can be a way of getting closer to Allah and gaining his favour.
- Some non-religious believers may argue that fasting today has no benefit because you are only making yourself suffer. They may argue that if the purpose of fasting is to support the poor, you can simply give to charity without the need to deprive yourself of food and drink.

Arguments in support of other views:
- Many Muslims would disagree with the statement because they believe Sawm is a duty from Allah and it is one of the Five Pillars of Islam. Many Muslims believe there are many benefits to Sawm, such as understanding the suffering of the poor. Fasting also helps Muslims realise their duty to help others – something they believe Allah wants them to do. For example, during Sawm many Muslims give more in Zakah.
- Some Muslims might argue that completing Sawm allows them to feel closer to Allah and reflect on Islamic teaching. While fasting, they may spend more time on inner reflection, which provides a source of spiritual strength to overcome the challenge of not eating and drinking.
- Many Muslims would disagree with the statement because Sawm has many spiritual benefits. For example, Muslims develop self-control and discipline by completing Sawm. Through Sawm, Muslims have to resist the temptation of eating and drinking and they may believe it teaches them to test themselves and not give in to this temptation.

32. Zakah and khums

1. C Khums
2. For example:
   - Muslims believe Zakah is a duty as it is one of the Five Pillars of Islam. They believe performing Zakah shows submission to Allah and is how he wants them to live. The Qur'an states the importance of performing Zakah, which Muhammad established.
   - Muslims also believe Zakah should be used to help the poor. This is a responsibility for every Muslim, as explained in the Qur'an. Surah 9:60 states how the money can be used. Zakah can be given to bring Muslims together as a community. It can also be used for freeing captives, helping those in debt and travellers, and for fighting in the name of Allah.
   - Muslims believe in order to achieve their reward in the afterlife they need to perform the duties given to them by Allah. One of these is to show care and concern for the poor, and one way this is achieved is through Zakah.

33. Hajj

1. Arguments in support:
   - Some Muslims may agree with the statement, arguing that although Hajj is one of the Five Pillars and it is expected that every Muslim completes it during their lifetime, the money to cover the expense of attending Hajj could be better used to help the poor, which is also a duty from Allah.
   - Although it is important to promote justice in the world (Surah 4:135), this can perhaps be better achieved through charity money rather than taking time out to complete a difficult, expensive and potentially dangerous pilgrimage. Some non-religious believers may see no purpose in completing Hajj as for them it is simply a journey. They may recognise that there is religious meaning in this journey for Muslims, but they may argue that the money can be better used to help the poor.

   Arguments in support of other views:
   - Many Muslims would strongly disagree with the statement, believing that as Hajj is the fifth Pillar of Islam, every fit and able Muslim has a duty to complete it. Completing this Pillar is thought to demonstrate submission to Allah and contribute to a Muslim being able to go to heaven in the afterlife.
   - Some Muslims save up for years to complete Hajj and some will even contribute to send one person to represent them if they themselves cannot afford to go. They may argue that it is a meaningful journey to trace the roots of Islam and walk in the footsteps of Muhammad.
   - Completing Hajj is a major achievement: it helps some Muslims to take time out of their normal lives to concentrate solely on Allah and develop a closer relationship with him. Although they may recognise that it is also important to spend money on helping the poor, many Muslims may argue that they do this already through Sawm and Zakah.

34. Jihad

1. For example:
   - Lesser jihad should be fought only as a last resort.
   - Lesser jihad should be fought only for a just cause.
   - Lesser jihad should be authorised by an accepted Muslim authority.
   - Lesser jihad should cause the least amount of suffering.
   - Lesser jihad should be fought with the aim of restoring peace and freedom.
2. For example:
   - One understanding of jihad is greater jihad, which is the inner struggle to be a better Muslim. Most Muslims believe this is the more important form of jihad. It can include the daily challenges for a Muslim of overcoming temptation in their lives, attending the mosque regularly, completing good deeds and studying the Qur'an.
   - One understanding of jihad is lesser jihad, which is a military struggle to defend Islam. This is carried out according to strict rules, such as only fighting as a last resort, fighting only for a just cause and only when authorised by an accepted Muslim authority.

35. Festivals and commemorations

1. A Ashura
2. Arguments in support:
   - Islam teaches that celebrations such as festivals are an important part of remembering past events and important people within Islam. For example, the festivals of Id mark important events in the Muslim calendar and remember events such as Id-ul-Adha, which recalls the willingness of Ibrahim to sacrifice his son to show submission to Allah.
   - Festivals in Islam allow all members of the ummah to be united in sharing the same beliefs and values. Festivals allow Muslims to come together, which may be particularly important in Britain today, where Muslims may feel isolated within a secular society.
   - Festivals are important for Muslims, to give them a sense of identity and belonging. As all Muslims celebrate events such as Id, festivals provide a focal point in the year for Muslims to come together to worship Allah.

   Arguments in support of other views:
   - Some Muslims may disagree with the statement. They may believe although festivals are an important way of demonstrating faith, the most important, central feature of Islam is Tawhid and belief in Allah. Although festivals demonstrate this belief, it may be considered more important to develop a personal relationship with Allah.
   - Although festivals may be seen to have a role within Islam, some Muslims may feel that celebrating through festivals is secondary to other religious actions, such as helping the poor or completing religious journeys such as Hajj.
   - Non-religious believers may feel that religious festivals are irrelevant today and that people should be able to come together as a community without relying on religious ideas to do so. They may criticise festivals such as Id-ul-Adha and Id-ul-Fitr as cruel, owing to the sacrifices of animals that take place.

Theme A: Relationships and families

Sex, marriage and divorce

36. Sexual relationships

1*. Arguments in support:
   - Many religious believers including Christians and Muslims believe pre-marital sex and adultery are wrong.
   - St Paul taught that sexual relationships before marriage are wrong and that 'neither the sexually immoral… nor adulterers… will inherit the Kingdom of God' (1 Corinthians 6:9–10). Many Christians therefore choose to take a vow of chastity until marriage.
   - Many Christians believe procreation is a key purpose of marriage and that only marriage provides children with a stable family unit in which to be raised.
   - Christianity teaches that adultery is wrong as it breaks the vows made in marriage (to be faithful until 'death do us part'). Adultery is also against one of the Ten Commandments ('You shall not commit adultery', Exodus 20:14).
   - Islam teaches that sex before marriage is wrong because sex is a gift from Allah that should take place only between married couples. The Hadith teaches: 'When a husband and wife share intimacy it is rewarded and a blessing from Allah.'
   - Muslims believe they will be rewarded if they 'keep themselves chaste' (Surah 24:33) until after marriage and that marriage provides a stable foundation within which children can be raised.

   Arguments in support of other views:
   - Some liberal Christians believe if a couple is in a long-term, loving relationship, a sexual relationship is a form of commitment and acceptable, provided they intend to get married in the future.
   - Currently, homosexuals cannot get married in a church unless the Christian denomination allows it. Some liberal Christians may argue that homosexuals should be allowed to have a sexual relationship as consenting adults outside of Church-approved marriage.

- Some non-religious believers may argue that consenting adults should be allowed to have a sexual relationship outside of marriage, providing it does not harm anyone else. They may argue that commitment can take many forms and that if a couple in a sexual relationship chooses not to marry and have children, this should be recognised as a relevant and acceptable form of commitment.

37. Sexual relationships

1 B Homosexual
2 For example:
Christianity:
- The Christian Church traditionally supports heterosexual relationships, as the Bible teaches that marriage is for one man and one woman. Genesis 2:24 states that a person leaves their father and mother and 'becomes one flesh' through marriage.
- Some Christians are more tolerant of homosexual relationships. The Bible teaches the importance of respect and some Christians believe this extends to all forms of relationships. They may argue that because the Bible teaches that 'all humans were created in the image of God' (Genesis 1:26), all forms of love should be celebrated.

Islam:
- Islam has strict views on relationships, believing that only heterosexual relationships (between a man and a woman) are allowed. This is because sex is an act of worship and a gift from Allah, the main purpose of which is procreation. Surah 24:2 talks about the need to punish homosexual relationships because they bring dishonour.
- Muslims believe sexual relationships before marriage are wrong because sex is a gift from Allah that should take place only within marriage and with the purpose of starting a family. Muslims believe they will be rewarded for staying chaste prior to marriage. For example, a Hadith describes a sexual relationship after marriage as a 'blessing from Allah'.

38. Contraception

1 A Family planning
2 For example:
- Many Christians/Muslims believe the use of contraception is wrong, as they believe God intends sexual relationships to be for procreation (having children).
- Many Christians/Muslims may argue that contraception could encourage casual sex, increasing the risk of sexually transmitted infections.
- The *Humanae Vitae* and some Islamic texts do not support the use of contraception.
- Some religious believers see some contraception methods as an early abortion, which goes against religious views of the sanctity of life.

3 For example:
- A religious couple may use contraception for family planning.
- A religious couple may use contraception if the birth of another child would put pressure on the family unit.
- A religious couple may use contraception if the mother's life were at risk with another pregnancy.
- A religious couple may use contraception if they believe that sex is also for pleasure and not just for procreation.
- A religious couple may use methods of contraception that do not go against God's teachings.

39. Contraception

1* Arguments in support:
- Islam teaches that the purpose of a sexual relationship within marriage is procreation and starting a family. As there is no possibility of procreation with most forms of artificial or permanent contraception, many Muslims do not support their use as it can be seen to go against the teachings of Islam.
- Many Catholic Christians believe every sexual act should be open to the possibility of conception, as this is what God intended and what Christianity teaches in Genesis 9:7; the use of contraception goes against this. Catholic Christians may also refer to the *Humanae Vitae*, which does not support the use of contraception.
- Some religious believers, including both Christians and Muslims, believe some forms of contraception could be viewed as an early abortion, which goes against the sanctity of life and so they may reject them.

Arguments in support of other views:
- Some Muslims believe if pregnancy were to risk the life of the mother or the well-being of the children in the family unit, it would not be against religion for contraception to be used as the mother's life is also seen as having value because it was created by Allah.
- Many Muslims believe the use of contraception within a married, committed relationship is sensible for family planning and therefore not against religion. They may suggest using non-permanent, natural methods of contraception, however, as these allow for the possibility of a pregnancy in future.
- Some Protestant Christians may argue that although the main purpose of a sexual relationship is procreation, another important purpose of sex is pleasure. Therefore, they may argue that using contraception means that a couple can have a meaningful committed relationship without worrying about unwanted pregnancies.

- Many non-religious believers see nothing wrong in the use of contraception. They may argue that sex can be just for pleasure and that it is a person's right to choose whether and when to have children. Using contraception supports this right.

40. Marriage

1* Arguments in support:
- Many Christians agree with the statement, believing that marriage is intended for life, as the vows made before God during the marriage ceremony are when a couple promises to be together until death.
- Christians believe marriage is a sacrament – a ceremony in which God is involved – so promises made to each other and to God should not be broken. This is shown in Mark 10:9 when it says: 'Therefore what God has joined together, let no one separate.'
- In Christianity, marriage is understood as a gift from God and part of God's plan for men and women to live together, so marriage should be 'for life'. Mark 10:6–9 talks of 'the two becoming one flesh' through the sacrament of marriage.
- Islam teaches that Allah created man and woman for each other and the Qur'an (Surah 24:32) teaches that Muslims should get married and not remain single.
- In Islam, marriage is seen as the correct context in which to raise children as Muslims. Marriage is seen as a legal contract between a couple and it is intended to be for life.

Arguments in support of other views:
- Christians may accept divorce in certain circumstances, for example if there has been adultery in the relationship or if one partner has abused the other. This is supported in the Bible, where Jesus states that adultery is a valid reason for ending a marriage (Matthew 19:8–9).
- Although Muslims are taught that marriage should be for life, they also recognise that relationships can go wrong and sometimes divorce is necessary. This is shown through guidelines for divorce in Islamic sources of authority such as the Qur'an. Most Muslims are supportive of remarriage as they believe marriage brings stability to the family unit and society, so they accept that marriage cannot always be for life.
- Non-religious believers may argue that if a marriage has broken down the couple should not be forced to stay together for life.

41. Marriage

1 For example:
- Christians/Muslims believe God/Allah intends for a married couple to have children.
- Christians/Muslims believe God/Allah intends marriage to be between a man and a woman.

- Christians believe marriage is a sacred union that is intended to be for life.
- Marriage in Islam is a legal contract that is intended to be for life.
- Islam allows polygamy for men.
- Muslims may have an arranged marriage.

2 For example:
Christianity:
- Christians believe a key purpose of marriage is to enjoy a sexual relationship and have children. For example, Genesis 1:27 gives the command: 'Be fruitful and multiply.' Marriage is seen to bring stability to society by the couple making a lifelong commitment to each other, which is seen as setting a good moral and social example. Mark 10:6–9 encourages this lifelong commitment: 'Therefore, what God has joined together, let no one separate.'
- Many Christians see marriage as providing companionship, friendship and support between husband and wife.

Islam:
- Islam teaches that Allah created man and woman for each other, so most Muslims believe the main purpose of marriage is to bring a man and a woman together in order to have children and start a family. The Qur'an (Surah 24:32) teaches that Muslims should get married and not remain single.
- Islam teaches that Allah intends marriage to allow for the sharing of love, companionship and sex between a man and a woman in a committed relationship. The Hadith teaches: 'When a husband and wife share intimacy it is rewarded and a blessing from Allah.'
- Marriage is seen to give stability to society. The Qur'an (Surah 49:13) talks about Allah creating males and females for each other so that they may know each other.

42. Different relationships

1 For example:
- In Christianity, cohabitation is disliked and not encouraged.
- In Islam, cohabitation is seen as unacceptable.
- Cohabitation may lead to sex outside marriage.
- A cohabiting couple may be less committed to each other than a married couple, who have made vows before God.
- Cohabitation does not provide the same stability for the family unit as marriage does.

2 For example:
Christianity:
- Traditional Christian teaching is against homosexual relationships as the Church teaches that one of the purposes of a sexual relationship is to procreate, and same-sex couples cannot have children naturally. Traditionally, the Christian Church does not support same-sex marriage as it is believed God intends marriage to be between a man and a woman.
- Some modern Christians challenge traditional Christian attitudes against homosexual relationships, believing that teachings on equality are important in Christianity and that all humans should have the same rights, including the right to be in a loving relationship.

Islam:
- Traditional Islamic teachings forbid homosexual relationships and do not recognise same-sex marriage. This is because Muslims are taught that homosexual relationships are not what Allah intends and are therefore wrong. Many Muslims may accept teachings from the Qur'an that say homosexual relationships are unnatural because they do not produce children naturally, which is a key purpose of marriage. Many Muslims believe homosexual relationships threaten the stability of Islamic society.
- A small minority of Muslims today challenge traditional Islamic teachings about homosexual relationships being wrong. They believe all loving relationships should be celebrated and recognised. For example, some practising Muslims in Britain have had a same-sex wedding.

43. Different relationships

1* Arguments in support:
- Most Muslims would agree with the statement as Islam traditionally forbids same-sex relationships. Islam teaches that Allah intends marriage to be between one man and one woman, to allow for procreation.
- Islam teaches that same-sex marriage is unnatural and against the will of Allah, so most Muslims would argue that same-sex marriage goes against religious teachings.
- Many Catholics would agree with the statement as Catholic teachings do not support homosexual relationships. The Bible states that God created man and woman for each other to procreate (Genesis 1:27). As homosexual couples cannot have children naturally, most Catholics do not agree with same-sex marriage.
- Some Christians in the Church of England would agree with the statement as they believe marriage should be between a man and a woman. Many ministers in the Church of England refuse to carry out same-sex weddings in a church for this reason.

Arguments in support of other views:
- Some Christians may disagree with the statement, believing it is important for religious people to support same-sex marriage. They may refer to religious teachings on equality and argue that all couples have the same rights to a loving relationship before God when making commitments to each other. One Christian denomination that campaigns for marriage equality is the Quakers, who officiate at same-sex marriage ceremonies.
- Many non-religious believers see nothing wrong with same-sex marriage, believing that all people deserve equality. Many believe if two people want to make the commitment of marriage to each other, they should be allowed to do so. They may argue that religious believers should support this right.
- In UK law it is illegal to discriminate, so all people of faith should be allowed to get married, whatever their sexual preference. Religions have a message of love and peace that suggests such discrimination is wrong.

44. Divorce and remarriage

1 For example:
- Divorce is not encouraged by religious believers.
- Christians and Muslims intend marriage to be for life.
- There are key teachings in Christianity and Islam against divorce.
- Divorce might be accepted by some Christians and Muslims, but only as a last resort.
- Religious believers may see divorce as acceptable when there has been adultery or one partner in the marriage is abusive.

2 For example:
Christianity:
- Catholic Christians do not accept remarriage because they do not recognise or allow divorce. They believe marriage should be for life, as stated in the marriage vows ('till death do us part'). If a Catholic does remarry, the marriage ceremony could not take place in a Catholic Church.
- Many Protestant Christians accept remarriage as they recognise that sometimes marriages do not work out. They may argue that marriage remains the best environment to provide stability for the family unit and so would support a divorced person getting married again to someone else. It is up to the individual vicar to decide whether a divorced person can be married in a Protestant Church. Reference may be made to Mark 10:9, which says 'Therefore what God has joined together, let no one separate.' This suggests that marriage should be for life.

Islam:
- Muslims are allowed to remarry after a divorce as marriage is seen as a social contract that can be broken and ended. Islamic teachings encourage Muslims to remarry in order to provide stability for the family unit. Reference may be made to Surah 24:32, which encourages marriage.

45. Divorce and remarriage

1 B Divorce

2   For example:
    - Many Christians/Muslims believe divorce is acceptable only as a last resort.
    - Many Christians/Muslims see divorce as disrespectful to God, as marriage is seen as a gift from God.
    - Divorce should be carried out in line with the guidelines given in holy books.
    - All forms of reconciliation should be tried before divorce is allowed.
    - Marriage is intended to be for life so divorce is not encouraged.
3   For example:
    - Remarriage may be encouraged to provide family stability.
    - Remarriage is acceptable if someone has been wronged in the relationship (adultery); they should not be prevented from finding happiness with another partner.
    - People can make mistakes and God is forgiving.
    - Divorce is sometimes necessary.
    - Happiness and companionship are important.

Families and gender equality

46. Families

1* Arguments in support:
    - Christians believe the family is important and may consider a nuclear family to be the ideal family unit, where children can be raised in a positive, stable and nurturing environment. They may feel that the nuclear family closely reflects the idea of family in the Bible. Christians also believe God made man and woman for each other, as taught in Genesis 2:24, so they could raise a family.
    - Islam teaches that the family is important and should be based on the relationship between a husband and his wife and their children. Muslims are taught that the husband and wife have special roles in the family unit as male and female. This suggests that some types of family (for example, single-parent and sex-same families) cannot fully complete these roles and will provide less stability. For these reasons they are not encouraged.
    - Some Christians/Muslims may believe there are potential issues with blended families as they are made from 'broken' marriages, and that single parents and same-sex families do not offer the same stability and support for children as nuclear families.
    Arguments in support of other views:
    - Some Christians believe it is more important to have a loving and stable family, whatever form that family takes. They may argue that love is a key idea in Christianity, as shown through Jesus' teachings.
    - Muslims often prefer to live as extended families rather than nuclear families, as caring for both older and younger family members is seen as important in Islam. This is taught in Surah 17:23, when Muslims are told to be kind to their parents. Many Muslims may feel that an extended family provides a more supportive, loving and stable environment in which children can be raised, where they can benefit from close relationships with grandparents and other relatives.
    - Non-religious believers may argue that a family where parents love each other and care for their children is more important than whether the parents are married or the type of family unit they live in.

47. Families

1   For example:
    - To provide stability in society.
    - To help children grow within a safe and loving environment.
    - To educate children.
    - To teach children morals.
    - To care for all family members, especially the elderly.
    - To raise children within the faith.
    - Christians/Muslims believe God intends for men and women to marry so that they can procreate (have children).
2   For example:
    Christianity:
    - The Bible teaches that each person in the family unit has a specific role to fulfil. Parents have a responsibility to love and care for their children while introducing them to the Christian faith; children are encouraged to obey and learn from their parents (Ephesians 6:1).
    - Christians believe the Bible teaches that all members of a family should be shown respect, for example 'Honour your mother and father' from the Ten Commandments (Exodus 20:10).
    - Many Christians believe it is more important to raise children in a loving family than the form the family takes. They may refer to Deuteronomy 6:6–7, which says that parents should teach children the commandments given from God.
    Islam:
    - Many quotes in the Qur'an talk about family and teach young people to have respect for their elders. Muslims traditionally support extended families, where several generations can live together and support each other, so that elderly members can be cared for.
    - Most Muslims believe family unity, support and care is what Allah intended for humans; Surah 49:13 highlights the family as important to Allah.
    - The Qur'an teaches that Muslim children should be 'kind to parents' (Surah 17:23) as they introduce their children to the Islamic faith. Muslim parents have distinct roles and one element of this is to share and raise their children within Islam.

48. Contemporary issues

1   D Gender equality
2   For example:
    Christianity:
    - Some parts of the Bible give a traditional view that God created women as 'helpmates' for men, as shown in Genesis 2:18, in which God states 'It is not good for the man to be alone. I will make a helper suitable for him.' Some Christians take this to mean that God intends for men to be head of the household and women to look after the home and family.
    - Many Christians today feel that a traditional understanding of men as providers and women as helpers or having to care for the home is outdated. They may argue that men and women have more equal roles in terms of working to earn money, doing household chores, and caring for and raising children. Reference may be made to Genesis 1:26, which states that both men and women were 'created in the image of God', suggesting they are equal.
    Islam:
    - Women in Islam are traditionally seen to hold the roles of raising the children, looking after the home and supporting their husbands. Sahih al-Bukhari 64:278 states 'The righteous among the women of Quraish are those who are kind to their young ones and who look after their husband's property.'
    - Some quotes from Islamic sources suggest that men and women were created equally but with different roles that were designed to support each other, suggesting that women's roles are equal (but different) to those of men. However, some quotes from the Qur'an, such as Surah 4:34, suggest that 'men are in charge of women' so women should obey men in all they do.

49. Contemporary issues

1   For example:
    - Traditional Islamic teachings accept polygamy.
    - In some Islamic countries, Muslim men may have up to four wives, but each wife has to agree to other wives.
    - Muslim women can only have one husband, as the paternity (father) of the child should be known.
    - Christians do not support polygamy.
2   For example:
    Christianity:
    - Exodus 20:10 states 'Honour your mother and father'. This could be interpreted as God intending that a family should include a husband and a wife. In this sense, same-sex parents are not supported by Bible teachings and are therefore seen by some Christians as wrong.
    - Some teachings in the Bible do not identify any gender for parents.

For example, Colossians 3:20 says 'children, obey your parents' and does not clarify the gender of the parents. This lends support to some modern Christians' claims that same-sex parenting is acceptable.

Islam:
- Muslims traditionally do not support same-sex parents, believing that the family should include a mother and a father. They look to traditional Islamic teachings that support this view, such as Surah 49:13, which includes a man and a woman being made by Allah for the purpose of procreation. Many Muslims believe this teaching suggests a family should not have same-sex parents.

50. Gender prejudice and discrimination

1* Arguments in support:
- There are many teachings in Christianity that support the view of equality between men and women in religious life. Galatians 3:28 states that all humans are equal before God.
- There are many examples of equality seen in the Christian Church. For example, women can now hold positions of authority, such as bishop, in the Protestant Church.
- Many Christian organisations promote and teach ideas of gender equality. Bible teachings include the instruction to 'love thy neighbour' and the example of Jesus, who helps and supports both women and men.
- Islam teaches that gender inequality and discrimination are wrong because Allah created all humans to be equal. From Surah 33:35, Muslims believe Allah rewards men and women equally so they will be judged in the same way after death, irrespective of gender.
- Many non-religious believers share the view that men and women are of equal value and should have equal rights and opportunities in all areas of life, including religious rights. Many UK laws also promote equal rights.

Arguments in support of other views:
- Some Catholic Church practices promote ideas of inequality between men and women. For example, the Catholic Church only allows men to hold the positions of bishop, priest, deacon and pope because Jesus was male.
- In Islam, teachings such as Surah 4:34, which states 'Men are in charge of women', suggest that although Allah created men and women equally, equality in religion is not expected. Many Muslims accept that men and women are suited to different roles and responsibilities.
- Some non-religious believers may argue that there are key differences between men and women that should be recognised in all aspects of life, including religion.

51. Gender prejudice and discrimination

1   D Gender prejudice
2   For example:
Christianity:
- Many Christians believe God created all humans to be equal. Bible teachings such as Galatians 3:28 stress that there is no difference between men and women as they are all the same before Jesus. Christians believe this tells them they should not treat men and women differently. For example, women can now hold positions of authority, such as bishop, in the Protestant Church.

Islam:
- Many Muslims believe gender discrimination is wrong as Islam teaches that Allah treats men and women equally and judges them in the same way after death. Surah 33:35 states that men and women will be judged on the Day of Judgement in the same way. As Muslims' beliefs and actions contribute to the quality of their afterlife, Muslims believe this is an argument for gender equality.

52. Relationships and families: Contrasting beliefs

1   For example:
Christianity:
- Catholics believe artificial methods of contraception, such as the Pill and condoms, are wrong as they prevent the main purpose of sex, which Catholic teachings state is to have children (procreation). Some Catholics are more accepting of natural forms of contraception, such as the withdrawal method, which still allow for the possibility of procreation.

Islam:
- Some Muslims view artificial methods of contraception as wrong, but believe natural forms of contraception can be allowed as they allow for the possibility of a child to be conceived if Allah wishes. This view is supported by Sahih al-Bukhari 62:136.

2   For example:
Christianity:
- Many Christians believe sexual relationships before marriage are wrong as this is the teaching of St Paul recorded in the Bible. Some Christians therefore take a vow of chastity before marriage.
- Some liberal Christians are more accepting of a sexual relationship before marriage, provided the couple are in a long-term, committed and loving relationship. If the couple intends to get married in the future, liberal Christians may view a sexual relationship as a form of commitment and a way of deepening the relationship.

Islam:
- Most Muslims view sexual relationships before marriage as wrong as sex is seen as a gift from Allah to be saved for a committed married couple. Muslims believe the Qur'an teaches them to save themselves for after marriage and many Muslims therefore take a vow of chastity beforehand.

53. Relationships and families: Contrasting beliefs

1   For example:
Christianity:
- Many Christians believe sexual relationships before marriage are wrong as this is the teaching of St Paul recorded in the Bible. Some Christians therefore take a vow of chastity before marriage.
- Sex may be seen as a gift from God that is intended for the purpose of procreation, so some Christians believe sex should be saved for after marriage, when the family unit can be established and children raised within the Christian faith.

Islam:
- Most Muslims view sexual relationships before marriage as wrong as sex is seen as a gift from Allah to be saved for a committed married couple. Muslims believe the Qur'an teaches them to save themselves for after marriage and many Muslims therefore take a vow of chastity beforehand.

2   For example:
Christianity:
- Traditional Christian teaching is against homosexual relationships as the Church teaches that one of the purposes of a sexual relationship is to procreate and same-sex couples cannot have children naturally. Traditionally, the Christian Church does not support same-sex marriage as it is believed God intends marriage to be between a man and a woman only.
- Some modern Christians have challenged traditional Christian attitudes against homosexual relationships, believing that teachings on equality are important in Christianity and that all humans should have the same rights, including the right to be in a loving relationship.

Islam:
- Traditional Islamic teachings forbid homosexual relationships and do not recognise same-sex marriage. Muslims are taught that homosexual relationships are not what Allah intended and are therefore wrong. Many Muslims may accept teachings from the Qur'an that say homosexual relationships are unnatural because they do not produce children naturally. Many Muslims believe homosexual relationships threaten the stability of Islamic society.
- A minority of Muslims today challenge traditional Islamic teachings about homosexual relationships being wrong and believe all loving relationships should be celebrated

159

and recognised. There have been a few examples of practising Muslims having a same-sex wedding.

Theme B: Religion and life
Origins and value of the universe

54. Origins of the universe

1* Arguments in support:
- Some Christians may agree with the statement, arguing that the biblical account in Genesis of the creation of the universe is the word of God. As the biblical account does not mention the Big Bang, and these Christians believe the Bible is true in all its detail as it was written by God, they argue that scientific explanations of the origin of the universe must be wrong.
- Some Muslims understand the account of creation given in the Qur'an literally, accepting it as the actual truth. They would argue that Allah created the universe exactly as the Qur'an states ('Allah is the creator of all things', Surah 39:62) and that anything that is not mentioned in the Qur'an (for example, the Big Bang) did not happen, so they would reject scientific explanations for the origins of the universe.

Arguments in support of other views:
- Some Christians believe scientific and religious explanations of the creation of the universe are both valid. They believe the Bible account of creation explains why the world was created and science explains how. They still believe God created the universe, as Genesis 1 says, but that he used the Big Bang to achieve this.
- Some Muslims would disagree with the statement, arguing that science does not challenge their belief in Allah's creation of the universe. Rather, they may believe scientific theories such as the Big Bang help to 'fill in gaps' in the Qur'an's account of creation and help them to understand how God works. Muslims may point to the fact that there are references in the Qur'an, such as 'we are its expander' (Surah 51:47), that could be referring to ideas such as the Big Bang.
- Non-religious believers may disagree with the statement, arguing that only scientific explanations of the origin of the universe are valid and that all explanations based on religious teachings in holy books should be rejected.

55. Origins of the universe

1. C Creation
2. For example:

Christianity:
- Some Christians, known as literalists, reject all scientific explanations for the origins of the universe, believing that only the Christian Creation story found in the Bible is true. Where there is conflict between Christianity and science, such as the belief that God created the universe ('In the beginning, God created the heavens and the earth', Genesis 1:1–2) and the scientific theory of the Big Bang, they will reject scientific explanations.
- Some Christians, known as non-literalists, see no conflict between Christianity and science. They accept the scientific theory of the Big Bang, believing that this was part of God's plan for the creation of the universe. They would argue that Genesis 1 is not a factual account and needs to be reinterpreted metaphorically.

Islam:
- Some Muslims take a literalist view, believing that when the Qur'an states 'Allah is the creator of all things' (Surah 39:62) this is literally true. They believe anything that is not mentioned in the Qur'an (such as scientific explanations including the Big Bang) did not happen, as the Qur'an contains the words of Allah.
- Some Muslims take a non-literalist view: they believe Allah created the universe and that he did so with a 'Big Bang', as scientific theory describes. Surah 51:47 talks of the idea of 'expansion', and some Muslims believe this is a reference to the Big Bang.

56. The value of the world

1. B Stewardship
2. For example:

Christianity:
- Christians believe God gave humans stewardship over the Earth, which is a responsibility to care for his creation and look after it for future generations. Reference may be made to Psalm 24:1, which says 'The Earth is the Lord's and everything in it.'
- Christians believe God gave humans dominion over the Earth, which means they have power over the world that should be used responsibly through caring for it. The Bible teaches that humans were 'made in the image of God' (Genesis 1:26) to care for his special creation.

Islam:
- Muslims believe the Earth does not belong to humans, but that Allah gave it to humanity as a gift and therefore it should be returned to Allah. They believe Allah will judge them after death on how they have cared for the world. Surah 35:39 says, 'It is He who has made you successors upon the Earth.'
- Muslims are taught that Allah made humans khalifahs (stewards) and gave them the responsibility to care for the universe. The Qur'an is clear that the Earth does not belong to humans and they are taking care of it. A Hadith says 'Allah has appointed you his stewards over [the Earth]'.

57. The value of the world

1* Arguments in support:
- Many Muslims strongly agree with the statement as they believe the Qur'an is clear that Allah is the creator of the world (Surah 39:62) and that it does not belong to humans but he has trusted people to care for it as khalifahs – caretakers.
- Islam teaches that Allah made the world as a gift for humans and that he will judge them after death on the way they have treated his creation.
- Christians are taught that God made humans stewards of the Earth. This means they should act as caretakers of the world for God and look after his creation. Many passages in the Bible reinforce this belief, such as Psalm 24:1 which talks of the Earth belonging to God.
- Genesis 1 talks about the responsibility of dominion that God gave to humanity. This means that although humans have power over the world including animals, they should take care of them because all life is sacred as God created it.
- Both Muslims and Christians believe that God's creation is amazing – it inspires them with awe and wonder. They accept that this means they have a responsibility to care for it and never abuse it.
- Non-religious believers might argue that, although they do not believe a God created the universe, humans should still look after the world because they have a responsibility to care for it for the next generation and to ensure that life, which is important, can continue. They would argue from a non-religious perspective but they might suggest that protecting the world is the morally right thing to do.

Arguments in support of other views:
- Some non-religious believers may argue that 'you only live once' and therefore we should make the most of our lives. They may feel no responsibility to care for the world.
- Some people might argue that the Earth can take care of itself and that human interference only makes things worse. They could argue that the Earth was around a long time before humanity ever existed.
- Some people might argue that caring for the Earth should be the job of those in power, such as politicians, and those who are best informed to do so, such as ecologists and science experts. The responsibility should not be shared with everyone.
- Some Christians might argue that the responsibility of caring for people and loving each other, a key teaching of Jesus, is more important than caring for the world.

58. The natural world

1. For example:
- Religious believers can help care for the world by church collections to

- support environmental projects.
- Religious believers can help care for the world by recycling.
- Religious believers can help care for the world by praying for the strength to care for the environment.
- Religious believers can help care for the world by avoiding creating waste.
- Religious believers can help care for the world by supporting environmental campaigns.

2 For example:
Christianity:
- Many Christians believe God gave animals to humans for the purpose of food, so they do not have a problem with animals being used for food. They may argue that animals should still be cared for while they are alive but that there is nothing wrong with eating them. They may quote Genesis 9:3, which says 'Every moving thing that lives shall be food for you.'
- Some Christian religious texts state that humans were 'made in the image of God' (Genesis 1:26) and to stand apart from animals, and were given dominion over the Earth. Many Christians therefore believe it is acceptable for people to use animals for food if they wish.

Islam:
- Many Muslims believe Allah created animals and gave them to humans to eat. They believe animals should be treated with kindness and respect but that they ultimately exist for the purpose of fulfilling human needs. Surah 40:79 says 'It is Allah who made for you the grazing animals upon which you ride and some of them you eat.'
- Muslims believe animals can be used for food but respect should be shown to them. Surah 2:60 says 'Eat and drink from the provision of Allah and do not commit abuse on the Earth, spreading corruption.' Muslims therefore kill meat according to halal rules, which they believe cause the animals as little pain as possible.

59. The natural world

1* Arguments in support:
- Some Muslims may agree with the statement. They may choose to be vegetarian and not eat meat, or they may be vegan and not eat or use any animal products. They may argue that all animals are part of Allah's creation as the Qur'an says 'it is Allah who made animals for you' (Surah 40:79) and they should be taken care of, and that transporting and killing them for food is not taking care of them.
- Some Christians may argue that as God gave humans stewardship over animals, this is also an instruction not to eat them. They may argue that as God made all creatures, caring for animals means treating them the same as humans. They may therefore choose to be vegetarian and not eat meat, or to be vegan and not eat or use any animal products.
- Some non-religious believers may agree with the statement. They may choose to be vegetarian and not eat meat, or to be vegan and not eat or use any animal products. This decision may be made for ethical reasons (and not religious reasons). For example, they may believe making animals suffer is cruel and unnecessary or they may argue that the meat industry disrupts fragile ecosystems and damages the environment.

Arguments in support of other views:
- Many Muslims might disagree with the statement, arguing that the Qur'an states that animals are part of Allah's creation and that Allah gave animals to humans for them to use and eat. For example, Surah 40:79 states that humans can ride cattle and use them for food.
- Many Muslims might argue that is fine to eat meat but only if strict rules about killing animals for food are followed. They may believe all meat should be halal (which means 'allowed'). This means it is killed in an appropriate way that does not cause suffering to the animal.
- Many Christians would disagree with the statement, arguing that eating animals is acceptable. They may refer to Genesis 9:3, which talks of God giving animals to humans for food ('Every moving thing that lives shall be food for you.')
- Some Christians might disagree with the statement, arguing that humans are special and superior to animals. They may refer to Genesis 1:26, which states that only humans were 'made in the image of God'. Many non-religious believers see nothing wrong with eating meat, though not for religious reasons. They may argue meat is a vital source of protein in the human diet. They may believe livestock animals are fine for human use as food, although they may argue that they should be killed humanely and not excessively so as disrupt important ecosystems.

Origins and value of human life

60. Origins of human life

1 C Evolution
2 For example:
Christianity:
- Some Christians believe it is possible to accept both scientific and religious accounts of the origins of humanity. They believe evolution was part of God's plan in creating humanity. They may argue that the origin of humanity through Adam and Eve, as described in Genesis 1 and 2, needs reinterpreting for modern life.
- Other Christians may argue that scientific theories such as the theory of evolution are incompatible with the biblical account of creation. They may therefore reject scientific explanations for the origins of humanity. They may argue the Bible does not mention evolution, but instead Genesis 2:9 explains how God created man from the dust of the ground and breathed life into him.

Islam:
- Some Muslims believe science offers more convincing explanations for the origins of humanity than the Qur'an does. They believe it is important to adapt the account in the Qur'an to reflect modern scientific theories such as evolution. For example, Surah 21:30 states that Allah created humans, and some Muslims believe Allah did this through evolution.
- Some Muslims take a literalist view, believing that when the Qur'an states 'Allah is the creator of all things' (Surah 39:62), this is literally true. They believe anything that is not mentioned in the Qur'an (such as scientific explanations including the theory of evolution) did not happen, as the Qur'an contains the words of Allah.

61. Origins of human life

1 For example:
- Muslims/Christians believe Adam and Hawa/Eve were the first humans.
- Muslims/Christians believe God created humans.
- Muslims/Christians believe humans were created from dust/clay.
- Muslims/Christians believe God planned and designed humans.
- Muslims/Christians believe humans were given roles and responsibilities from God.
- Christians believe the first woman (Eve) was made out of the first man's (Adam's) rib.

2 For example:
Christianity:
- Some Christians believe the scientific theory of evolution is incompatible with Bible teachings and therefore reject it. They believe that as the Bible in Genesis 1 states that God created humans – first Adam out of the dust and then Eve from Adam's rib – this is exactly how humans were created.
- Other Christians believe the theory of evolution does not contradict the biblical account in Genesis 1 of the creation of humans. They believe God used evolution in order to achieve his goal of creating humanity. They would argue that the Creation account is not factual but symbolic, yet contains important truths such as God creating humans.

Islam:
- Most Muslims believe evolution theory does not conflict with Islamic teachings about the creation of humanity. The Qur'an makes it clear that Allah is the origin of human life, yet Muslims believe he may have used evolution. They believe science provides a more accurate account of this process and that

scientific understanding can help to deepen knowledge of religious truths contained in the Qur'an.
- Some Muslims believe evolution directly contradicts the account in the Qur'an of the creation of humans. They take the account in the Qur'an literally so, when it says that humans were made from clay, they believe this is exactly how it happened. They therefore reject the scientific theory of evolution because it gives a different explanation of human origins.

62. Sanctity and quality of life

1* Arguments in support:
- Some Christians may agree with the statement, believing that although all life is sacred, a person's quality of life is important. They may apply Jesus' teachings on compassion to situations where a person is suffering, such as someone with a degenerative disease, to suggest it may be more compassionate to end their suffering, if that is what they wish, by ending their life.
- Some non-religious believers may agree with the statement. They may argue that if a person is suffering they should have the right to choose to end their life. Although they may believe each life is special and has value, they are unlikely to agree with any religious arguments about the need to endure suffering or the sanctity of life.

Arguments in support of other views:
- Most Christians would disagree with the statement as Christianity teaches that suffering and pain do not stop life being valuable. Many Christians would therefore argue that, although it is important to ensure that everyone has a good quality of life, someone's sanctity of life is more important. They may refer to teachings such as Genesis 1:27 ('So God created mankind in his own image') or Exodus 20:13 ('You shall not murder').
- Most Christians believe all life is a gift from God worthy of respect and protection. They may argue that ending someone's life because their quality of life is poor is unacceptable and disrespectful to God.
- Both Christians and Muslims believe God is loving and caring. Although they accept that people may have to suffer, both religions teach that God would not give someone more than they can cope with in terms of suffering in their lives.
- Most Muslims recognise the need to ensure a person's quality of life is good. However, they do not accept the ending of life under any circumstances. They believe life is sacred and that only Allah can decide how long each person's life lasts; this is not for humans to decide. They may view suffering as a test from Allah and argue that someone's quality of life is never a reason to decide to end a life.

63. Sanctity and quality of life

1   B Sanctity of life
2   For example:
- Muslims/Christians believe life is sacred because Allah/God created it.
- Muslims/Christians believe life is sacred because all life has equal value.
- Muslims/Christians believe life is sacred because humans were given souls.
- Muslims/Christians believe life is sacred because humans were given special responsibilities from God.
- Muslims/Christians believe life is sacred because humans were 'made in the image of God'.

3   For example:
- Quality of life is not a reason to end life.
- Suffering has a purpose.
- Only Allah/God can decide how long life lasts.
- Any poor quality of life is a test from Allah/God.
- Allah/God does not give someone more than they can cope with in terms of quality of life.

64. Abortion and euthanasia

1   For example:
- Some Christians/Muslims believe abortion is wrong as life is a sacred gift from God/Allah.
- Some Christians/Muslims believe abortion is wrong as life begins at conception.
- Some Christians/Muslims believe abortion is wrong as all life (even potential life) has value.
- Some Christians/Muslims believe abortion is wrong as it against the commandment 'Do not kill'.
- Some Christians/Muslims believe abortion is wrong as Allah/God has a plan for every human.

2   For example:
Christianity:
- Many Christians believe suffering has a purpose from God. They may look to the example of Job in the Bible, who suffered but did not lose his faith. They may believe suffering can be relieved through hospice care and so therefore euthanasia is not necessary.

Islam:
- Many Muslims believe suffering is a test from Allah that has a special purpose. They may believe only Allah can give and end life, and that no one else has the right to so.

65. Abortion and euthanasia

1* Arguments in support:
- Some Muslims believe abortion is wrong and should never be allowed, as all life is special and sacred because Allah created it. They would also argue that abortion disrespects Allah's gift of life and may be punished in the afterlife.
- Some Christians (including Catholic Christians) believe abortion should not be allowed. They may accept that life begins at conception so abortion could be seen as murder, which is forbidden by the Ten Commandments (Exodus 20:13 states 'You shall not murder'). Many Muslims and Christians believe Allah/God has a plan and purpose for each human life. Abortion would prevent God's will from being carried out and so it should never be allowed.

Arguments in support of other views:
- Some Christians and Muslims recognise that, although life is sacred, abortion should sometimes be allowed, such as when a pregnancy occurs because of rape or where the life of the mother is at risk.
- Many Muslims believe ensoulment (when the soul enters the body) does not happen until 120 days after conception. Therefore, abortion before this time may be acceptable in some circumstances.
- Some non-religious believers claim abortion is a personal choice (it is the mother's right to choose) and should be an option because the rights of the mother outweigh the rights of the child as the child is not a person until birth. They may recognise that life is special and should be respected, but they would not have any concerns about going against God's will.

66. Death and the afterlife

1   A Afterlife
2   For example:
Christianity:
- Christians believe the resurrection of Jesus shows there is life after death. John 3:16 says that those who believe in Jesus will achieve eternal life with God in heaven ('whoever believes in him shall not perish but have eternal life').
- Christians believe Jesus taught there was an afterlife. Jesus said 'My father's house has many rooms' (John 14:2), suggesting that Christians can be with God in the afterlife.
- Christians believe in heaven and hell in the afterlife. They believe God will judge each person on their actions in this life and that, in order to go to heaven after death, they need to follow Jesus' example. John 11:25 says 'I am the resurrection and the life. The one who believes in me will live, even though they die.'

Islam:
- Islam teaches that Allah has full control over life and death and that all humans will face Allah's judgement in the afterlife. Many Muslims live each day of their life with this belief in mind. Reference may be made to Surah 39:70, which talks of humans being judged by Allah.
- Muslims are taught that good deeds will be rewarded and bad deeds will be punished in the afterlife. They accept belief in heaven (al-Jannah) and hell (Jahannam), which is detailed in Surah 28:61.

67. Death and the afterlife

1* Arguments in support:
- Belief in the afterlife is important to Muslims. They believe Allah is watching and will judge them on the way they have behaved: Surah 39:70 states that Allah is aware of every person's thoughts and actions. Muslims believe Allah's judgement determines whether they go to heaven (al-Jannah) or hell (Jahannam).
- The Qur'an tells Muslims what heaven and hell are like. It gives vivid descriptions, especially of the pain and torture of hell. As Muslims want to avoid going to hell, they try to live as they think Allah wants them to, with awareness that they will be judged after death.
- Belief in the afterlife is important to Christians. It guides them on how to live on Earth, as they want to spend their afterlife in heaven and will be afraid of being sent to hell if they do wrong.

Arguments in support of other views:
- Non-religious believers may strongly disagree with the statement, as they may believe death is the end and there is no afterlife. Therefore, they will be more concerned with making the most of their earthly life.
- Some Muslims may disagree with the statement. They may argue that constantly thinking about the afterlife is not how Allah wants them to live. They may believe Allah created the world for them to enjoy, as shown through Surah 2:60, when it says about eating and drinking from the provision of Allah. Therefore, they may believe Muslims should focus on enjoying their lives today while following Allah's rules.
- Some Christians may disagree with the statement. They may trust that they can be with God in heaven in the afterlife based on Christian teachings in the Bible; for example, John 11:25 says 'The one who believes in me will live, even though they die.' Many Christians may prefer to concentrate on living a full life as God intended, focusing on doing good in the world and spreading God's love rather than spending too much time thinking about the afterlife.

68. Religion and life: Contrasting beliefs

1 For example:
Christianity:
- Some Christian teachings suggest that God gave humans dominion (power) over animals, which many feel means that humans have a responsibility to care for animals. This would include not testing unnecessarily on animals.
- Many Christians believe unnecessary testing on animals is wrong as humans have the duty of stewardship. They may believe, however, that if testing on animals can help to save human lives then it is acceptable.

Islam:
- Muslims believe animals are important as they were created by Allah and should not be abused or exploited. Some Muslims believe this means animals should not be tested on.
- Many Muslims accept testing on animals if it helps to save human life, as Islam teaches that humans are at the top of Allah's creation.

2 For example:
Christianity:
- Some Christians do not accept abortion as they believe life is sacred because God created it. The Bible teaches 'You shall not kill', which is a commandment from God. As Christians believe life begins at conception and is a gift from God, abortion is always wrong.
- Other Christians believe there are times when abortion, although not encouraged, is the 'lesser of two evils'. In cases of rape or where a child may be born severely disabled, they may argue that it is kinder and more compassionate to allow an abortion.

Islam:
- Many Muslims do not accept abortion as all life is sacred and special as God created it.
- Many Muslims believe life begins at ensoulment (when the soul enters the body around 120 days after conception), so abortion may be considered acceptable to some Muslims before this time.
- Some Muslims believe if the mother's life is at risk abortion should be allowed as her life has value and purpose (sanctity of life) and she is already alive.

69. Religion and life: Contrasting beliefs

1 For example:
Christianity:
- Some Christians believe there are times when abortion, although not encouraged, is the 'lesser of two evils'. In cases of rape or where a child may be born severely disabled, they may argue that it is kinder and more compassionate to allow an abortion.

Islam:
- Many Muslims believe life begins at ensoulment (when the soul enters the body around 120 days after conception), so abortion may be considered acceptable to some Muslims before this time.
- Some Muslims believe if the mother's life is at risk abortion should be allowed as her life has value and purpose (sanctity of life) and she is already alive.

2 For example:
Christianity:
- Many Christians would not support the legalisation of euthanasia because they believe life is special as it was created by God and has a purpose. They believe God would not make a person suffer more than they can manage and that it is not a human's place to 'play God'.

Islam:
- Most Muslims would not support the legalisation of euthanasia, believing it to be murder and against Allah. Surah 2:156 says 'we belong to Allah', and many Muslims understand this to mean that only Allah can take life, making euthanasia always wrong.

Theme C: The existence of God and revelation

Philosophical arguments for and against the existence of God

70. The existence of God

1 B First Cause argument
2 For example:
Christianity:
- The Design argument tries to prove that God is omnipotent (all-powerful). God had the power to design the world so it had everything that humans would need within it. Genesis 1 describes God having the power to create the universe and everything within it.
- The Design argument tries to prove that God is omnibenevolent (all-loving). God took care with the design of the world and especially humans. Genesis 1:26 describes God creating humans in his image, giving them a soul and responsibilities such as stewardship.

Islam:
- Muslims believe the Design argument shows that Allah is omnipotent (all-powerful). His power is seen through the careful way he is believed to have designed the universe and the world within it, taking care to do it properly. Surah 2:164 refers to a 'One True God... the Lord of all creation'; many Muslims believe this offers proof that Allah exists and is powerful enough to have designed and created the world.

71. The existence of God

1 For example:
- The Design argument supports accounts in the holy books about the creation of the universe.
- The Design argument supports belief in the existence of Allah/God.
- The Design argument provides evidence of design that can be seen in the world.
- The Design argument supports the scientific theory of evolution.
- The Design argument supports understanding of the nature of Allah/God as omnipotent, omniscient and omnibenevolent.

2 For example:
Christianity:
- Christians believe St Thomas Aquinas created three versions of the First Cause argument that offered three ways of showing that God exists because he created the universe.

Aquinas argued that the evidence of cause and effect shows that the universe must have a first cause and this had to be God. The book of Genesis in the Bible reinforces this belief by stating that God created the world in six days, with a seventh day of rest.
- Christians also believe the First Cause argument shows the nature of God: omnipotent through the power he has to create the universe and benevolent through the care he took in creating the universe.

Islam:
- The First Cause argument can be seen in the Islamic cosmological argument called 'the kalam', put forward by Al-Ghazali in the 12th century, which states that as everything has a cause, the universe must have a cause. Surah 79 supports the First Cause argument as it describes how Allah created the world.
- Muslims believe the First Cause argument shows that Allah exists as well as describing what he is like. For example, Allah was able to create the universe because he is omnipotent; he took care in creating the universe because he is omnibenevolent. This is reinforced by Qur'anic accounts of the creation of the universe such as Surah 39:62, which says 'Allah is the creator of all things.'

72. Miracles

1. For example:
   - Jesus walking on water.
   - Jesus feeding a large crowd of people.
   - The resurrection of Jesus.
   - Noah and the floods.
   - Muhammad meeting Allah in heaven.
   - The revelation of the Qur'an.
2. For example:
Christianity:
   - Christians believe miracles prove the existence of an all-powerful being who is involved in the world. For example, Jesus performing healing miracles or walking on water in the Bible demonstrate God's power.
   - Christians believe miracles show that God is omnibenevolent: he cares for his creation. The resurrection of Jesus in the Bible shows the miracle of life after death that is available to Christians. John 3:16 states 'For God so loved the world that he gave his one and only Son, that whoever believes in him shall not perish but have eternal life.'

Islam:
   - Miracles are important to Muslims as the Qur'an makes it clear that Allah is able to perform miracles if he wants to. One example of a miracle described in the Qur'an is Muhammad meeting Allah in heaven, showing the power of Allah and that the revelations that Muhammad experienced were real.

73. Miracles

1. C Agnostic
2. For example:
Christianity:
   - Some Christians believe miracles prove God is omniscient as he must be watching the world to be able to intervene and help humans. This can be seen in examples of people surviving a near-death event (such as a fall from an aeroplane) that humans cannot explain. Christians may argue that such an event is a miracle from God.

Islam:
   - Miracles are important to Muslims in showing that God is omnibenevolent and cares for his creation by acting to help humans. This can be seen through examples such as the miracle of Nuh surviving the flood or Muhammad being taken to heaven to meet Allah, which helped to confirm his faith and belief in Allah.

74. Evil and suffering

1* Arguments in support:
   - Some Christians may agree with the statement, believing that, even though we may not know what the purpose of suffering is, it is important to accept our suffering as part of God's will. They may argue that suffering may be needed to allow humans to grow and develop, and that God has prepared a way for our salvation. They may refer to the example of Job from the Bible, who suffered and had his faith tested and yet never lost faith in God. Also, the Book of Psalms states that the purpose of evil and suffering is to give people the opportunity to follow Jesus' example and live as God intended.
   - Many Christians believe the presence of evil and suffering in the world helps humans to develop compassion and love, and therefore get closer to God. For example, Christians can work to reduce the amount of suffering in the world by supporting others through charity or volunteer work.
   - Some Christians would agree with the statement, arguing that God gave people free will and sometimes people choose to turn away from God and commit acts of evil. This explains why evil and suffering exist in God's world. Therefore, it is possible to still believe in God and accept evil and suffering.
   - Many Muslims would agree with the statement as Islam teaches that Muslims should turn to Allah through prayer and charity when they are suffering. Muslims believe suffering is a test of faith in Allah and that Allah will judge them in the afterlife on how well they pass this test.
   - Some Muslims may agree with that statement on the basis that Allah must have a reason for there being evil and suffering in the world. However, he is so great that humans cannot possibly understand this reason. They may argue that Muslims should accept suffering if it is the will of Allah (Inshallah).

Arguments in support of other views:
   - Many non-religious believers may use the fact that evil and suffering exists in the world as evidence that God does not exist, as a caring God would not let his creation suffer.
   - Some Christians and Muslims may find that their faith is challenged by the presence of evil and suffering in the world. Some believers may even lose their faith altogether.

75. Evil and suffering

1. B Atheist
2. For example:
   - It challenges the idea of God being all-loving (omnibenevolent.
   - It challenges the idea of God being all-powerful (omnipotent).
   - It challenges the idea of God being all-seeing and all-knowing (omniscient).
   - It challenges the idea of God existing.
3. For example:
   - Christians/Muslims believe they can help others by doing charity work.
   - Christians/Muslims believe they can help others by praying for those who are suffering.
   - Christians/Muslims believe they can help others by accepting that life is a test and that suffering has a purpose.
   - Christians/Muslims believe they can help others by forgiving those who hurt others.
   - Christians/Muslims believe they can help others by developing characteristics such as love and compassion.

76. Arguments against the existence of God

1. For example:
   - The Big Bang offers an alternative explanation to God creating the world.
   - Science may be considered more reliable than religion.
   - Science may be considered more relevant than holy books.
   - Evolution contradicts God creating humans.
2. For example:
Christianity:
   - Some Christians believe science does not pose a challenge to belief in God because science and religion together explain how the world came to exist. The Big Bang explains how life began, whereas the Creation account in Genesis explains that God is the creator of all life – that is, God created the Big Bang in Genesis 1:1–2.
   - Some Christians believe science (the theory of evolution) and religion (the Creation story in the Bible) can together explain the origins of humanity. Christians maintain that God created humans (Genesis 2:7) but that he used evolution to do this. They

may take a non-literal interpretation of the Bible to show there is no conflict between these ideas.

Islam:
- Many Muslims believe science does not pose a challenge to belief in God. They may accept that science offers more believable explanations than religious accounts, which they may argue need updating and should not be taken literally. They may refer to Surah 21:30, which states that Allah created humans, and they may claim that the scientific theory of evolution explains how Allah did this.

77. Arguments against the existence of God

1* Arguments in support:
- Some literalist Muslims may agree with the statement, arguing that all scientific explanations should be rejected because they are against Islamic teachings and a threat to beliefs about Allah being the sole creator of the universe. They may argue that as the Qur'an offers the words of Allah, only what is stated there must be true.
- Some literalist Christians may agree with the statement. They may argue that it is wrong to question God's existence and they may view the Bible as providing the only true account of creation. They may respond to science by rejecting it completely as it threatens their beliefs about God creating the universe.
- Some non-religious believers may agree with the statement because they can see no common ground between religion and science. They may argue that science provides reliable evidence based on observation and that religion is based on subjective feelings, and that its teachings about God creating the universe are therefore false and should be rejected.

Arguments in support of other views:
- Some Muslims may disagree with the statement, believing there are many similarities between the Qur'an and scientific explanations. They may point to Surah 51:47, which talks of the idea of 'expansion'. Some Muslims believe this is a direct reference to the expansion caused by the Big Bang when Allah created the universe.
- Many Muslims would disagree with the statement, believing that scientific explanations give them a better understanding of Allah and his creation. They may argue that science further develops teachings in the Qur'an and helps to 'fill the gaps' where things are not fully explained in the Qur'an.
- Many Christians see no conflict between the existence of God and scientific accounts. They may believe that together, science and Christian accounts provide a complete account of how God created the universe. They may argue that religion explains why (that is, that God created the universe) whereas science explains how (that is, the theories of the Big Bang and evolutionary theory). They may argue that it is possible to reinterpret traditional religious accounts of creation to reflect modern scientific understanding.

Nature of the divine and revelation

78. Special revelation: Visions

1 D Hymns
2 For example:
- Visions are important to Christians/Muslims because they allow messages from God/Allah to be passed on.
- Visions are important to Christians/Muslims because they are how God/Allah reveals himself to humanity.
- Visions are important to Christians/Muslims because they help people get closer to God/Allah.
- Visions are important to Christians/Muslims because they help humans understand God/Allah better.
- Visions are important to Christians/Muslims because they show that God/Allah cares for his creation.

3 For example:
- Paul/Saul and his miracle of conversion.
- St Bernadette seeing the miracle of the image of Mary.
- Moses parting the Red Sea.
- Mary's miracle of being told she would be the mother of Jesus.
- Muhammad and his miracle of having the Qur'an revealed.

79. Special revelation: Visions

1* Arguments in support:
- Some Muslims may believe there are better sources of revelation of Allah than visions, such as the Qur'an, which is a direct form of revelation of Allah and provides guidance on how he wants Muslims to live their lives.
- Some Muslims accept that visions happen, as Allah is all-present and has the power to intervene in the world, yet they may not see visions as contributing any reliable knowledge of Allah. They may believe having faith in Allah does not require proof of his existence and that visions do not provide reliable evidence of what Allah is like.
- Muslims are taught that Allah is transcendent, so humans are limited as to what they can really 'know' about him. Therefore, while many Muslims believe it is important to develop a relationship with Allah and to 'know' him in key ways (such as loving and forgiving), they may argue that no visions or any other method of revelation, can help them to fully know Allah.
- Some Christians may place less emphasis on visions as a way of 'knowing' God. They may accept that visions are just one method of revelation and that there are many other sources of revelation, such as the Bible as God's word. Miracles do not allow a person to 'know' God as they may not understand the message being given.
- Non-religious believers do not accept the existence of God so they will offer alternative explanations for visions. They may believe a person is hallucinating, ill or taking stimulants such as drugs. They do not see visions as a source of knowledge of God.

Arguments in support of other views:
- Many Muslims believe visions are a good way of 'knowing' Allah as they are a personal and often individual experience of him. This can be seen in the examples of Musa and Mary. They may point out that many people associated with Islam, including Muhammad, had visions and therefore they are a good source of knowing him.
- Many Christians would argue that visions as personal revelation do help a person to understand and know God better. There are many examples in Christianity of key figures, including Saul/Paul and St Bernadette, receiving visions from God that offered important messages or gave them a better understanding of him.

80. General revelation

1* Arguments in support:
- Many non-religious believers think there are logical, non-religious explanations for any experience described as 'revelation of God'. They may argue that someone who claims to have had a revelation of God is probably under the influence of stimulants such as drugs or alcohol, or is hallucinating, and that there is no evidence to prove God's existence.
- Some Christians may agree with the statement to some extent, believing that not all types of revelation are equally valid. They may claim that there is 'room for error' with some types of revelation, such as miracles or nature, as they involve a person's private interpretation of what has happened. Direct forms of revelation such as the Bible may be held to be more reliable.
- Some Muslims may agree with the statement in part, arguing that some forms of revelation hold more value than others or that those experiencing revelations such as miracles or visions may misinterpret what has happened. They may argue that Allah is too great to be revealed to normal humans and that this is why he chose prophets to be his messengers.

Arguments in support of other views:
- Most Christians would argue that revelation is communication from God and shows what God is like. They may argue there are many types

of revelation that can be trusted, including scripture such as the Bible, nature (which shows God's creation) and Jesus' example and teachings found in the Bible.
- Most Muslims would believe general revelation through the Qur'an, prophets and nature is excellent evidence for belief in God. They may believe people who claim to have had revelation of God are not mistaken; rather, they believe God passes on important messages in this way.
- Most Christians and Muslims would argue that many religions are founded on revelation, for example by God/Allah revealing himself through holy books, and for this reason revelation should be accepted as reliable.

81. General revelation

1 B Miracles
2 For example:
   - Through prophets such as Muhammad/Ibrahim/Noah/Abraham.
   - Through scripture and holy books such as the Bible/Qur'an.
   - Through nature.
3 For example:
   - Lack of evidence.
   - Explained by the use of stimulants.
   - Could be hallucinations.
   - Could be misinterpreted.
   - God's ideas in revelation could contradict each other.

82. The existence of God and revelation: Contrasting beliefs

1 For example:
   Christianity:
   - Many Christians believe nature provides good evidence of God as they accept that God created the world and believe the complexity of the world shows God's power and loving nature. They may argue that the Design argument provides good support for nature as general revelation because it suggests an all-powerful, all-knowing, eternal designer (God).
   - Some Christians believe that as the Christian account of creation is found in the Bible, this is good supporting evidence for revelation of God through creation.
   Islam:
   - Most Muslims believe nature is an important form of revelation of Allah. His creation shows them what he is like and reveals his characteristics, for example that he cares for his creation and has the power to create something amazing. Through this, Muslims can understand Allah better.
2 For example:
   Christianity:
   - Some Christians believe visions are direct revelations of God that may include important messages, such as those God gave to St Paul and Abraham. They may believe visions help them get closer to God and understand him better.
   - Some Christians believe miracles are not the best form of revelation of God as people can be unreliable witnesses and misinterpret an experience they believe to be from God. Some Christians may prefer direct forms of revelation, such as the Bible, believing this to be a more reliable form of revelation than miracles.
   Islam:
   - Some Muslims accept that visions happen but do not place great emphasis on them in proving that Allah is real or confirming his characteristics of omnipotence and omnibenevolence. Rather, they place greater emphasis on other sources of revelation of Allah, such as the Qur'an, which is seen as direct revelation given to Muhammad, or the prophets themselves, who gave important messages to humanity.
   - Some Muslims place great emphasis on visions because Muhammad himself experienced them. The Qur'an was revealed to Muhammad through a vision of the angel Jibril and he also saw Allah in heaven, which helped to confirm his faith.

83. The existence of God and revelation: Contrasting beliefs

1 For example:
   Christianity:
   - Many Christians believe miracles reinforce the characteristics of God, such as his omnipotence and omnibenevolence, and therefore believe miracles are good evidence for belief in God. Examples such as the miracles of Jesus, the resurrection of Jesus or modern-day miracles show that God cares for and loves his creation.
   Islam:
   - Many Muslims accept that Allah performs miracles to act within the world and show his love and care for the world. They believe Allah performed miracles such as revealing the Qur'an to Muhammad so that humans know he is close to them.
   Non-religious:
   - Many non-religious believers hold that miracles are simply the result of people misinterpreting events that are natural. They may look to the use of stimulants or medical conditions to explain scientifically why they happen.
   - Many non-religious believers will point to conflicting accounts of miracles to suggest that they are not real. They will argue that people misinterpret what they believe they are experiencing and, because they cannot explain it any other way, look to God to provide an explanation.
2 For example:
   Christianity:
   - Many Christians believe God's divine nature is revealed through the specialness of the world he created. For example, God's power can be seen through the many amazing things he created.
   - Some Christians accept the Design argument that says, as God created and designed the world, so God's existence is shown by the existence of the natural world. For many Christians, the world is evidence of God's existence. For example, God's power and love is shown through the rising of the sun, the cycles of nature, and the diversity of the plant and animal kingdoms.
   Islam:
   - Many Muslims believe Allah reveals himself through the natural world. They believe nature is perfect as Allah is its creator and Allah is perfect. They look to examples of how the world works successfully, such as the tides coming in and out and the sun rising and setting, to show this.
   Non-religious:
   - Many non-religious believers claim that nature does not provide evidence of God's existence. They may argue that the universe can be explained by scientific theories such as the Big Bang and evolution. They may not believe nature shows what God is like; they may accept that the world came about by chance rather than from the intervention of a divine being. Indeed, they may argue that God does not exist.

Theme D: Religion, peace and conflict

Religion, violence, terrorism and war

84. Peace and justice, forgiveness and reconciliation

1 For example:
   - Christians/Muslims believe God/Allah is just, so humans should be too.
   - Christians/Muslims believe seeing everyone as equal shows justice.
   - Christians believe Jesus taught that we should treat others as we would like to be treated.
   - Muslims believe Shari'ah law has strict rules about justice and acting fairly.
   - Muslims believe the Five Pillars of Islam support ideas of justice, e.g. Zakah (sharing wealth).
   - God/Allah made the world to be fair and just.
   - God/Allah judges people in the afterlife on how they have treated others.
2 For example:
   Christianity:
   - Jesus taught about the importance of forgiveness. For example, forgiveness is a key idea in the Lord's Prayer: 'Forgive us our trespasses as we forgive those who trespass against us.'
   - Christians believe they should try to follow the example of Jesus, who forgave those who crucified him. Jesus'

final words while on the cross were: 'Father, forgive them for they know not what they are doing' (Luke 23:34).
- There are many Christian teachings on forgiveness, such as the Parable of the Prodigal Son (Luke 15:11–32), which is based on ideas of forgiveness and reconciliation: the father forgave his son, even though he had wasted his inheritance.

Islam:
- Muslims believe Allah is forgiving and merciful and that they should act in this way towards others too; this is stated in Surah 64:14. Islam teaches that Muslims will be judged after death on how they have behaved towards others so it is important to be forgiving.
- Islam teaches that peace is what Allah intends for the world and Muslims believe forgiveness and reconciliation help to achieve this, as described in Surah 41:34.

85. Peace and justice, forgiveness and reconciliation

1* Arguments in support:
- There are many examples of ideas of peace being put into action within Islam, including the way Muslims greet each other. Indeed, the word 'Islam' is derived from the root of the word 'salaam', which means peace. Therefore, many Muslims may argue that if everyone applied Islamic teachings, peace could be achieved.
- Christianity teaches about the importance of forgiveness and shows people how they should work to forgive those who wrong them. Luke 6:37 states 'Forgive, and you will be forgiven'. Many Christians might therefore believe if everyone lived their lives putting Christian teachings into action, everyone could live together peacefully.
- There are many teachings on the importance of peace within all religions. For example, Islam teaches that Allah created and intended for the world to be peaceful. In the Qur'an, Surah 25:63 states that people should use words of peace towards each other. Christians follow the example of Jesus: 'I have told you these things, so that in me you may have peace' (John 16:33).

Arguments in support of other views:
- Many religious believers, including Muslims and Christians, may argue that although religion teaches ideas of peace, it may be impossible to put these teachings into practice throughout the world as some conflict is always inevitable and religion cannot solve this.
- Non-religious believers may argue that religion actually causes conflict rather than brings peace to the world. They may feel that religious disagreement is at the root of many conflicts in the world. They may also give examples of abuses or terrorist acts carried out in the name of religion to show that religion neither teaches nor brings about peace.

86. Violence and terrorism

1 B Terrorism
2 For example:
- Many Christians/Muslims believe acts of violence against people, such as terrorism, are wrong because God/Allah created life so it is sacred.
- There are many religious teachings on the importance of peace in the Bible/Qur'an.
- Violence goes against the teachings of Jesus/Islam.
- Christianity/Islam encourages reconciliation, not violence.

3 For example:
- Most Christians/Muslims believe the use of violence is wrong.
- Christian/Islamic teachings support peace, not violence.
- Some Christians may be pacifists and not support violence.
- Many Christians/Muslims may feel they have a duty to work for peace.
- Most Christians/Muslims believe God intended for a peaceful world.
- Some Christians/Muslims recognise that in some cases violence and war may be necessary to secure peace (for example, if they are under attack), but only after all peaceful methods have been tried first.

87. Violence and terrorism

1 For example:
Christianity:
- Christians believe the use of violence is wrong because Jesus taught 'Blessed are the peacemakers' (Matthew 5:9), meaning that those who act with peace towards others are favoured by God.
- Christians believe the use of violence is wrong as they have a duty from God to work for peace. Some may be pacifists and believe conflict should be solved peacefully rather than turning to violence.

Islam:
- Muslims believe using violence is wrong because Islam is a religion of peace.
- Muslims believe Allah is merciful and forgiving, therefore they should try to behave this way towards others.
- Muslims believe the servants of Allah are those who try to show peace towards others.

2 For example:
Christianity:
- Christians do not support terrorism because it threatens human life, which is sacred because God created it 'in the image of God' (Genesis 1:26).
- Christians do not support terrorism because it goes against Christian teachings that promote peace: Jesus taught 'Blessed are the peacemakers' (Matthew 5:9).

Islam:
- Most Muslims believe terrorism is wrong and use Islamic teachings of peace to show why. For example, Surah 8:61 promotes ideas of working together for peace rather than fighting through acts of terrorism.
- A small minority of Muslims use quotes from the Qur'an to justify terrorist acts. For example, Surah 9:5 suggests it is acceptable to use violence to attack those who are against Islam.

88. War and Just War theory

1* Arguments in support:
- Many Christians would agree with the statement, as they support ideas of peace and do not believe war is acceptable. They may refer to the many teachings in the Bible that support working together for peace, including teachings from Jesus on reconciliation and forgiveness.
- Some Christians choose to be pacifist, so would not support any use of violence, including fighting in war.
- Most Christians believe in the sanctity of life: all life is sacred as God created it. As war threatens and takes life, they may not support it.
- Islam is a religion that supports peace and non-violence, so Muslims may refer to teachings such as Surah 2:108 ('Enter absolutely into peace') or Surah 49:10 ('make settlement between your brothers') to argue that war is always wrong.
- Some non-religious believers may agree with the statement, arguing that war is wrong because it risks harm to innocent lives. Although they do not make reference to any religious teachings, they may argue that life is special because humans only have one life and deserve to live in peace.

Arguments in support of other views:
- Some Christians may believe that, although it is important to always work for peace in the world, war is sometimes necessary. They may refer to Just War theory, which gives criteria for how war should be fought and under what conditions.
- Some Muslims may believe some passages in the Qur'an suggest that war is permitted in certain circumstances, but only as a last resort when all other methods have failed. Surah 2:190 says: 'Fight in the way of Allah those who fight you', suggesting that war may be acceptable in cases of self-defence or to defend Islam.
- Some non-religious believers may feel that war is necessary at times in order to fight for a better world. For example, they may refer to the importance of Britain going to war with Nazi Germany in 1939 when Germany invaded Poland. They may argue that avoiding war weakens a country and makes it more vulnerable to being taken over by hostile forces. As they do not believe in God or an

afterlife, they may argue that it is up to humanity to fight to make life as good as it can be.

89. War and Just War theory
1. D Just war
2. For example:
   - The Bible/Qur'an teaches the use of violence/war is wrong.
   - War threatens innocent life.
   - War damages God's/Allah's creation.
   - Peace, not violence, is the way to be close to God/Allah.
   - God/Allah will punish those who harm life.
3. For example:
   - Some Christians/Muslims believe war may be necessary to achieve peace, but only as a last resort after all peaceful methods have been tried first.
   - Some teachings from Christian and Islamic holy books suggest war is acceptable when it is an act of defence, when it is fought fairly and when the aim is to bring peace.

90. Holy war
1. For example:
   - Christians/Muslims generally believe war is wrong as the Bible/Qur'an teaches messages of peace between all people.
   - Some Christians may be pacifist and believe war is always wrong.
   - Some Christians/Muslims may believe holy war is acceptable as 'God is on their side'.
   - Some Christians believe there is support for holy war in the Bible when Moses is told to take vengeance.
   - Some Muslims believe holy war is justified if defending the religion of Islam.
   - Some Muslims believe holy war can be used as a form of defence.
2. For example:
   Christianity:
   - Some Christians believe a few passages from the Old Testament in the Bible which suggest that war may sometimes be the right action to take. This includes passages that suggest fighting and taking vengeance on behalf of God is acceptable. For example, God told Moses to 'take vengeance on the Midianites' (Numbers 31:1–2).
   - In the past, such as during the Crusades in the Middle Ages, Christians fought in holy wars because they believed God wanted them to defend Christian holy sites from other religions. In the 11th, 12th and 13th centuries, Christians went on Crusades to 'free' the holy places in Palestine. They based their actions on teachings such as Matthew 10 ('whoever loses their life for my sake will find it'), understanding this to mean that those who fight in the name of God will be rewarded.

Islam:
- For Muslims, holy war – known as Harb al-Maqadis – is only acceptable if it is done to defend the religion of Islam. Muslims follow Muhammad, who was involved in holy wars.
- Teachings such as Surah 9:5 tell Muslims when it is acceptable to 'kill', 'capture' and 'beseige' non-Muslims.
- Muslims are taught that holy war is only acceptable under certain conditions. These include it must be for reasons of defence; war can only be declared by a religious leader and only as a last resort; effort must be made to avoid harming innocent civilians; war must not be fought to gain land.

91. Holy war
1* Arguments in support:
   - Some Christians are pacifists who believe war and the use of violence can never be justified. Other Christians may be against the use of violence, even a holy war, because Christian teachings and Jesus' example promote peace. Bible teachings that support this view include 'Blessed are the peacemakers' (Matthew 5:9) and 'Love your enemies and pray for those who persecute you' (Matthew 5:44).
   - Some Muslims may believe war and violence are always wrong and not justified for any reason. They may refer to Muslim teachings such as Surah 25:63 ('And the servants of the Most Merciful are those who walk upon the earth easily, and when the ignorant address them [harshly], they say [words of] peace'.) Some non-religious believers may argue that going to war in defence of a religion is no different to going to war to gain land or remove a dictator. Although they do not have religious beliefs, they may believe life is precious and that the loss of life and human suffering caused by all types of war is wrong.

   Arguments in support of other views:
   - Some Muslims believe holy war is different to war generally because it is fought in the name of Allah and therefore blessed by Allah. They may argue that as holy war follows set criteria, it is fair and only happens for just reasons and as a last resort. Some Christians may argue that some passages in the Bible, such as Numbers 31:1–2, in which God tells Moses to take revenge on the Midianites, suggest that holy war is different to others wars because it has God's support. Some Christians may also argue that because holy war is only justified according to strict religious criteria, it is better than war in general. Some non-religious believers may argue that holy war is worse than war in general because religious reasons should not be used to justify war. They may argue that those who believe war is 'what God wants' are mistaken because there is no God. Therefore, any war justified on religious grounds is based on illusion.

92. Pacifism
1. D Pacifism
2. For example:
   Christianity:
   - Some Christians support pacifism because they believe that, as God created all humans, there is a part of God in every human and so they should oppose anything that could harm people, including violence. This reflects Christian belief in the sanctity of life and Bible teachings, including 'You shall not murder' (Exodus 20:13) and 'So God created mankind in his own image' (Genesis 1:27), which suggests human life is special.
   - Many Christians believe they should support pacifism as Jesus taught 'Love your enemies and pray for those who persecute you' (Matthew 43:44).
   Islam
   - There is some support for pacifism or passive resistance in Islam, although Islam is not a pacifist religion, as many Muslims support the idea of holy war. Support for pacifism can be found in some Muslim teachings, including Surah 5:28, which states that violence should not be faced with violence. There are many other teachings of peace in Islam, such as teachings on the importance of reconciliation and working together to achieve peace using non-violent protest.

93. Pacifism
1. D Peaceful protest with no violence
2. For example:
   - Jesus taught about the importance of peace in the Bible.
   - Some religious believers refuse to fight in wars as they believe it is important to work for peace in the world.
   - God wanted a peaceful world.
   - Conscientious objectors support pacifism, believing life is sacred and should be protected at all costs.
   - Violence is wrong as it threatens innocent life.
3. For example:
   - Both pacifism and Christianity/Islam uphold religious beliefs about the sanctity of life.
   - There are many religious teachings that support peace.
   - Jesus taught 'blessed are the peacemakers'.
   - Religious believers believe God wants them to oppose anything that harms people.
   - Religious believers believe God wants them to work for peace.
   - Religious believers believe they have a duty to work for forgiveness and reconciliation between people in the world.

Religion and belief in 21st-century conflict

94. Religion as a cause of conflict

1. For example:
   - There is a high loss of life.
   - Danger of these weapons.
   - Damage to the environment.
   - It is against the teachings of peace.
   - The conditions of Just War theory are not met.
2. * Arguments in support:
   - Most Christians believe the problems of WMD outweigh any of the benefits. They may argue that the damage, destruction and high loss of life from WMD mean their use cannot be justified under any circumstances. They may also be concerned about the risks of storing them. They may refer to Christian teachings on the sanctity of life, which state that as God created all life, it is special and should not be threatened.
   - Some Christians, such as Quakers, choose to be pacifist and so do not support the use of violence, including WMD. They may refer to Christian teachings of peace that suggest the use of violence is unacceptable. For example, Jesus taught 'Love your enemies and pray for those who persecute you' (Matthew 5:44) and 'all who draw the sword will die by the sword' (Matthew 26:52).
   - Islam teaches ideas of peace so most Muslims would not support the use of WMD under any circumstances. They may believe Allah's creation should be taken care of and not harmed in any way so it is wrong to harm innocent life and cause environmental destruction through the use of WMD.
   - Many non-religious believers oppose the use of WMD on humane grounds rather than because of any religious beliefs. They may feel that no life should be threatened by the use of such powerful and destructive weapons.

   Arguments in support of other views:
   - Some religious and non-religious believers may recognise the benefits of having WMD as a deterrent, even if they do not actively support their use. This deterrent may deter other nations from starting a war, instead finding peaceful solutions to conflict.

95. Religion as a cause of conflict

1. A Weapons of mass destruction
2. For example:
   Christianity:
   - Some Christians recognise the value of having WMD as a deterrent to avoid wars starting and conflicts escalating into war. This may help to bring about peaceful solutions; peace is a key teaching of Jesus.

   Islam:
   - Some Muslims believe WMD are wrong, even as a deterrent, because of the tremendous risk of death and destruction – even in storage. They may argue that all life is sacred as Allah created it and that all Muslims have a duty from Allah to care for the Earth. Therefore, the risks of harm from WMD are too great to be acceptable.

96. Religion and peacemaking

1. C Peace
2. For example:
   - Christians/Muslims may donate money or goods.
   - Christians/Muslims may complete volunteer work.
   - Christians/Muslims may take in refugees and give them a place to live.
   - Christians/Muslims may speak out against the suffering victims of war have faced.
   - Christian/Muslim charities may work to help victims of war rebuild their lives.
3. For example:
   - Nelson Mandela, Betty Williams, Martin Luther King, Malala Yousafzai, Muhammad Ali.

97. Religion and peacemaking

1. * Arguments in support:
   - Christian organisations such as CAFOD and Christian Aid are able to reach people in areas affected by war and offer immediate medical care and support. Many Christians therefore feel that the best way to help victims of war is by providing financial support to charities such as CAFOD and Christian Aid, especially as they may feel there is little they can do to support such victims personally.
   - Many Muslims would believe charity organisations such as the Red Crescent Movement and Islamic Relief are best placed to help those affected by war as they are able to get aid to those that need it and provide medical care and other resources. Although most Muslims feel they have a duty from Allah to help others, they may feel there is little they can do to support victims of war personally other than giving to charity (Zakah), which is one of the Five Pillars of Islam.
   - Many Christians look to teachings from the Bible to understand how they can best help and support others in the world, including victims of war. The Parable of the Sheep and the Goats (Matthew 25:31–46) teaches that we have a duty to help others, whereas Matthew 7:12 teaches us to 'do to others what you would have them do to you'. Some Christians may believe charity organisations are the best way of putting such teachings into action. Likewise, Muslims may look to teachings in the Qur'an and Hadith, such as Hadith 13, which says 'None of you truly believes until he wishes for his brother what he wishes for himself' to justify why charity organisations may be the best method of helping victims of war.
   - Many non-religious believers would agree with the statement that charity organisations can best help victims of war. They may recognise that charities often have access to the best resources, including medical aid, and they can pay for what is needed through the donations they receive so can achieve more than individuals. Therefore, donations are the best way to help.

   Arguments in support of other views:
   - Some Christians or Muslims may argue that, although charities make a big contribution to supporting victims of war, individuals can help as well and perhaps can have a bigger impact. They may look to the examples of significant Christians or Muslims such as Martin Luther King, Betty Williams, Malala Yousafzai and Muhammad Ali, who all worked for peace, raised awareness of the difficulties facing those who are victims of war and violence and tried to help them. Individual actions such as taking an individual refugee into your home could make a huge difference to that individual's quality of life.
   - Some Christians and Muslims may argue that, although support can be given to victims of war, only they themselves can work to change their lives once this support is given. Therefore, it could be argued that the biggest change comes from the efforts victims make themselves to restart their lives.
   - Some non-religious believers may feel that only governments can really make a difference to help victims of war by working to end conflict. They may also argue that governments are best placed to provide foreign aid to war-torn countries and that it is more important, therefore, for individuals to campaign for government intervention in foreign wars than to give money to charity.

98. Religion, peace and conflict: Contrasting beliefs

1. For example:
   Christianity:
   - Many Christians believe the use of violence is wrong, as Christianity has many teachings on peace. Some Christians choose to be pacifist because they believe they are following Jesus' teachings by doing so.

   Islam:
   - Many Muslims believe the use of violence is wrong. Islam is a religion of peace, forgiveness and reconciliation that teaches Allah is merciful and that Muslims should

follow Allah's example by finding peaceful solutions to problems rather than resorting to violence.

2   For example:
    Christianity:
    - Some Christians, such as Quakers, choose to be pacifist, arguing that the use of violence can never be justified. They may look to Bible teachings such as 'You shall not kill' to support this viewpoint.
    Islam:
    - Islam is not traditionally understood as a pacifist religion, although it promotes ideas of peace, because within Islam it is recognised that violence is sometimes necessary to defend Islam.

99. Religion, peace and conflict: Contrasting beliefs

1   For example:
    Christianity:
    - Many Christians believe the use of violence is wrong, as Christianity has many teachings on peace. Some Christians choose to be pacifist because they believe they are following Jesus' teachings by doing so.
    - Many Christians view Jesus as a pacifist as many of his teachings are about peace. They believe putting teachings such as 'Blessed are the peacemakers' (Matthew 5:9) into action is following his example and living their lives as God intended.
    - The Christian denomination of the Quakers is opposed to all violence and supports pacifism. Many Quakers are conscientious objectors; they believe war is always wrong.
    Islam:
    - Although Islam is not a pacifist religion, it is a religion of peace, forgiveness and reconciliation. Islam teaches that Allah is merciful and that Muslims should follow Allah's example by finding peaceful solutions to problems rather than resorting to violence.
    - The Qur'an has some teachings in line with pacifism. Surah 5:28 talks of not facing violence with violence, which some Muslims argue supports pacifism.

2   For example:
    Christianity:
    - Many Christians believe violent protest is wrong because the Bible teaches that we should work for peace and reconciliation between people ('Blessed are the peacemakers'). Some Christians choose to be pacifist because they believe they are following Jesus' teachings. For example, Luke 22:49–51 describes how Jesus spoke out against violence during his arrest in the Garden of Gethsemane when some of his disciples attacked a guard, cutting off his ear.
    Islam:
    - Some Muslims believe the use of violence may sometimes be justified when protesting in order to secure peace in the long term. Surah 2:190 justifies the use of violence as a last resort, especially when defending Islam, when it says 'Fight in the way of Allah'.

Theme E: Religion, crime and punishment
Religion, crime and the causes of crime
100. Good and evil intentions and actions

1   A Evil
2   For example:
    - Christians/Muslims believe good actions will allow them to be rewarded in the afterlife by God/Allah.
    - Christians/Muslims believe good actions include living life as God/Allah intended by rules such as the Ten Commandments.
    - Good actions for Christians/Muslims may include helping others and doing charity work.
    - Muslims believe Allah is always watching them so will see their good actions in life.
    - Muslims believe after death Allah will judge them on both their actions and their intentions.
3   For example:
    - Suffering is part of God's/Allah's plan.
    - Suffering is a test of faith.
    - Suffering teaches someone to be stronger.
    - Suffering can help someone develop characteristics such as compassion and caring for others.
    - Some suffering is due to human abuse of free will.

101. Good and evil intentions and actions

1* Arguments in support:
    - Many Muslims would agree with the statement as Islam teaches that intentions should be sincere and actions should be for the right reasons. Islam is understood by Muslims to mean 'submission to Allah', and many Muslims believe this should be their intention behind every action.
    - Teachings from the Qur'an state that Allah will judge people after death on their actions and their intentions. This is why they believe both are equally important.
    - Many Christians would agree with the statement as the Bible states that the intentions behind a person's actions are just as important as their actions. For example, a person who helps others through charity work because they believe all humans deserve proper care and love can be seen to be acting for the right reasons. By contrast, someone who does charity work to get praise for themselves would be acting for the wrong reasons. Christians believe God will judge them after death on both their thoughts and their deeds (actions), as both are equally important.
    - Many non-religious believers may refer to UK law, which states that the intention behind a crime determines the nature of the crime. Therefore, premeditated (planned) murder carries a longer prison sentence than murder carried out on the 'spur of the moment' as a crime of passion. Many non-religious believers would therefore argue that a person's intentions are just as important as their actions.

    Arguments in support of other views:
    - Some Christians and Muslims may argue that as God/Allah gave humans free will, a person's intentions are more important than their actions. This is because free will and choice are linked first to intention and then actions follow afterwards. Without the intention, there would be no action.
    - Some Christians, Muslims and non-religious believers may argue that sometimes a person's good intentions may inadvertently lead to a bad action. For example, a person may give someone food not realising it will cause their death by choking. They would argue that, in this case, their intention was more important as they did not realise what the outcome would be.
    - Some non-religious believers may argue that actions are more important than intentions because you cannot actually know what a person's intentions are. A person may perform a good action for selfish or wrong intentions. Therefore, you can only really judge a person on their actions.

102. Reasons for crime

1* Arguments in support:
    - Some religious believers may believe that people sometimes turn to crime for understandable reasons and therefore deserve our support. For example, some people turn to crime because they are poor and desperate, through mental illness or addiction, or are part of a family where crime is common. Many Christians and Muslims believe people struggling in these ways should be helped and that punishment would only make their situation worse. Christians believe God gave humanity the duty of caring for others, as seen in the teaching to 'love your neighbour' (Mark 12:31). Islam teaches that Muslims have a duty to help reduce the causes of crime and they use Zakah (charity) as one way of doing this.
    - Many non-religious believers may agree with the statement because they think the education and rehabilitation of criminals is more effective than punishing them. They may recognise that some crimes are committed because of mental illness, addiction or

poverty, so support is more effective than punishment, based on humane grounds, rather than on any religious belief.
- Christianity teaches that forgiveness is important and that people need to work to forgive others rather than to punish them. For example, the Bible states 'Do not judge and you will not be judged. Do not condemn and you will not be condemned. Forgive and you will be forgiven' (Luke 6:36–37). Many Christians would therefore argue that the education and rehabilitation of criminals is far more important than punishing them.

Arguments in support of other views:
- Some Christians and Muslims would disagree with the statement as they believe all crime requires fair punishment to achieve justice – so the victim gains retribution and the criminal can reform. Many Bible teachings talk of the importance of fairness. For example, Isaiah called on people to behave justly towards others (Isaiah 58:6–7). Muslims believe punishment establishes peace and justice on Earth, as Allah intended, and the Qur'an gives specific instructions for punishing particular crimes. This shows the importance of punishment as a means of reforming the criminal, so the crimes are not repeated.
- Some non-religious believers may argue that punishment is necessary to deter criminals from committing crimes again and that helping them only makes criminals think they can 'get away with' their crimes. They may also argue that it is important that the victims of crime see that those who have wronged them are punished for their crimes.

103. Reasons for crime

1 For example:
- Many Muslims/Christians see punishment as important because a key purpose of punishment is to bring about a peaceful society as Muslims/Christians believe this is what Allah/God intends for the world.
- Punishment is a deterrent to other people who may commit the same crimes.
- Punishment gives the criminal a chance to change their behaviour.
- Punishment allows a victim to feel they have been repaid for the crime committed to them.

2 For example:
Christianity:
- The Bible teaches in Romans 13:1 that all people should follow the law of the country in which they live. If a crime is committed, the person should accept the punishment given by the laws of that country.
- Christians teach that all humans have the potential to sin and commit crimes. This is because God gave them free will, as seen in the story of Adam and Eve from Genesis, and sin is seen as part of human nature.

Islam:
- Muslims believe crime is a distraction from Allah and therefore wrong. The Qur'an teaches in Surah 5:90 that to be successful and please Allah, good Muslims should avoid committing crimes.
- Muslims believe they have a duty to help those who are affected by crime. They believe the ummah is important. It includes all Muslims, so everybody should be cared for and looked after.

104. Types of crime

1 D Hate crime
2 For example:
- Christians believe murder is against one of the Ten Commandments, which says 'You shall not kill.'
- Both Christians and Muslims believe murder is against the sanctity of life.
- Both Christians and Muslims believe murder is against the teachings of holy books.
- Both Christians and Muslims believe murder can be given the most severe punishment, including the death penalty.
- Both Christians and Muslims believe God/Allah punishes those who kill in the afterlife.

3 For example:
- Killing another person.
- Stealing from another person.
- Lying to others.
- Hate crimes.
- Treating other people unfairly.
- Adultery.

105. Types of crime

1* Arguments in support:
- Some Muslims may agree with the statement as Muslims in Britain have been the victims of hate crimes in recent times. As a result of some terrorist attacks being incorrectly linked to Muslims in general, many British Muslims have been on the receiving end of Islamophobia, such as graffiti, verbal abuse and physical assaults. They may therefore believe hate crimes deserve the most severe punishments.
- Some Christians may agree with the statement because they are concerned about hate crimes in society today. They may look to Bible teachings that suggest everyone deserves equal treatment, such as 'love your neighbour as yourself' (Matthew 22:39) and 'There is neither Jew nor Greek, slave nor free, male nor female, for you are all one in Christ Jesus' (Galatians 3:28). They might argue that the severity of hate crimes means they should have harsher punishments.
- Some non-religious believers may argue that hate crimes should have the strongest punishments because they can lead to genocide, where a certain group of people is deliberately killed. They may refer to the example of Nazi Germany, where hate crimes against Jewish people eventually led to the Holocaust, in which some 6 million Jews were murdered.

Arguments in support of other views:
- Some Muslims/Christians may argue that murder is a more serious crime than hate crimes and so deserves the strongest punishment. They may argue that all crimes require appropriate and just punishments and more serious crimes deserve more severe punishments to ensure justice is served. They may see murder as the worst crime because it destroys life, which is sacred.
- Christians may refer to religious teachings such as 'your bodies are temples of the Holy Spirit' (1 Corinthians 6:19) and 'Do to others as you would have them do to you' (Luke 6:31). Muslims may refer to Surah 4:135: 'be persistently standing firm in justice, witnesses for Allah, even if it be against yourselves or parents and relatives'.
- Non-religious believers may argue that murder and physical or sexual assaults that leave victims suffering for life are the worst types of crime and so they should receive the most severe punishments. They may argue that some types of hate crime, such as vandalism, are minor in comparison to other types of hate crime, such as physical assault, so the type of hate crime needs to be taken into account before deciding on the most appropriate punishments for the crime committed.

Religion and punishment

106. Punishment

1 For example:
- One aim of punishment is for criminals to realise what they have done wrong and to change their behaviour.
- One aim of punishment is reformation.
- One aim of punishment is protection of society.
- One aim of punishment is retribution.
- One aim of punishment is deterrence.
- One aim of punishment is so victims gain justice.

2 For example:
Christianity:
- Christians believe it is important for criminals to be punished when they have committed a crime as they believe God is just and fair and so they should try to be too. Punishing a criminal fairly for a crime allows for justice, which helps the victim feel the criminal has 'paid' for their actions. Exodus 21:25 ('an eye for an eye, a tooth for a tooth') suggests that people should be punished appropriately for their crimes.

- Christians believe criminals should be given the opportunity to reform themselves and change their behaviour. This could mean educating them or giving them opportunities such as a job, financial support if they are living in poverty or help to overcome an addiction. Jesus taught about agape love, as seen through the Parable of the Good Samaritan (Luke 10:25–37).

Islam:
- Islam teaches about the importance of protecting society. Punishment such as putting a criminal in prison is seen as important to achieve this protection. Muslims believe Allah is just and that they should therefore strive to be just in their treatment of others. Reference may be made to Surah 4:135, which says 'be persistently standing firm in justice, witnesses for Allah, even if it be against yourselves or parents and relatives'.
- Muslims believe Allah is forgiving and he wants them to also be forgiving towards others. Punishment allows a criminal to realise what they have done is wrong and change their behaviour so they can be forgiven. Reference may be made to Surah 4:26–27, which states that criminals should be given a chance to reform through punishment.

107. Punishment

1. D Revenge
2. For example:
Christianity:
- Christianity teaches that reformation of criminals is important. Christians are taught to follow the example of Jesus in demonstrating agape love towards criminals and giving them time to reform. This is seen as putting the teachings of Jesus (such as the Parable of the Good Samaritan) into action.
- Christianity teaches about the importance of forgiving others, as seen in the Lord's Prayer taught by Jesus. Even on the cross, Jesus forgave those who put him to death, saying 'Father, forgive them, for they do not know what they do' (Luke 23:34). Therefore, most Christians believe they should be forgiving and help criminals to reform.

Islam:
- Muslims believe the reformation of criminals is a key aim of punishment as Islam teaches about the importance of giving people a second chance and allowing them to change their behaviour. Surah 26 talks about Allah forgiving those who have committed crimes and the importance of guiding them to 'good practices' – that is, giving criminals the chance to reform – provided they are sorry for their crimes.
- Islam teaches in the Qur'an that Allah is merciful. Surah 64:14 says 'Allah is forgiving and merciful'. Therefore, Muslims are encouraged to also show mercy towards others and allowing a criminal time to reform is seen as merciful.

108. The treatment of criminals

1* Arguments in support:
- Some Christians and Muslims may partly agree with the statement in terms of all people, including those accused of committing crimes, being given a fair trial and the opportunity to defend their actions. Christians believe justice is very important. A key teaching of the Bible is that all humanity 'are one in Christ Jesus' (Galatians 3:28). Surah 4:135 teaches Muslims that justice and fairness should be considered at all times.
- Christianity teaches that criminals should have some equality with other people in society. For example, Christians believe corporal (physical) punishment or torture is wrong, so they would not support this for anybody, including criminals. They may believe that although someone may have done wrong, the punishment given should be humane as all life is sacred and should always be respected.
- Some Muslims would not support the use of physical punishment or torture for criminals, believing that all people should be respected and given the same rights and dignities. This is because they believe Allah created all human life and it should be respected at all times.

Arguments in support of other views:
- Many Christians would disagree with the statement, believing that although criminals deserve to have some human rights such as the rights to freedom from torture, to dignity, and to food and water, they must lose some of their rights and freedoms. For example, those in prison should be treated respectfully, but their access to society and freedoms should be limited as this seems just and fair to the victims of the crime.
- If a criminal was treated the same as everyone else, this would be unfair to the victims of their crimes. Many Christians and Muslims would therefore argue that the criminal has done wrong and deserves to be punished according to the laws of the country.
- Some non-religious believers may disagree with the statement. They may argue that for serious crimes, such as fraud, drink driving and murder, it is essential that criminals are imprisoned so that society is protected and criminals are given a chance to reform. They may argue that treating criminals the same as other people in society would suggest that criminals can 'get away with' their crimes and this would be morally wrong.

109. The treatment of criminals

1. B Imprisonment
2. For example:
Christianity:
- Christianity teaches that, although criminals have done wrong, they deserve to keep their basic human rights such as the right to food, water and medical care. They may refer to Galatians 3:28, which states that all humans are the same before Jesus, to argue that criminals deserve to have their human rights respected.
- Many Christians believe criminals should have a fair trial where they are able to put forward a defence and explain their actions. John 7:51 teaches that all criminals should have a chance to defend themselves in front of a fair trial.

Islam:
- Most Muslims believe criminals should be treated with dignity and still have their basic human rights respected. As they have committed a crime, they may deserve to have their freedom taken away by being imprisoned, yet they are still human and part of Allah's sacred creation so they deserve to be treated with respect at the same time as justice is achieved. Surah 4:135 teaches Muslims that justice and fairness should be considered at all times.

110. Forgiveness

1. For example:
- Forgiving someone when they have done something wrong allows for reconciliation, which is an important teaching in Christianity.
- Forgiveness brings reconciliation.
- Forgiveness follows the example of Jesus who forgave others.
- God/Allah is forgiving.
- Forgiveness allows everyone to move on from the act.
- Forgiveness follows teachings in holy books such as the Bible and the Qur'an.

2. For example:
Christianity:
- Christians believe it is important to forgive criminals because Jesus died on the cross to bring forgiveness and reconciliation between God and humanity. It is therefore important to Christians to follow the example of Jesus and forgive those who wrong us. Christians believe the Lord's Prayer teaches that we should forgive criminals as we would like to be forgiven, meaning that if Christians want forgiveness for the things they do wrong, they have to try to forgive others.

Islam:
- Muslims believe Allah is forgiving so they should try to be also. The Qur'an teaches that if someone is genuinely sorry for what they have done wrong, they should be forgiven.

- Islam is a religion of peace and teaches Muslims to live in harmony with each other. This can be achieved through forgiving people, including criminals, for the things they have done wrong.

111. Forgiveness

1. A Reformation
2. For example:
   Christianity:
   - Christianity teaches that Christians should try to forgive others when they have wronged them, even if this is difficult to do, as God will help them. Mark 11:29 instructs: 'Be kind and compassionate to one another, forgiving each other.' Christians believe Jesus died on the cross to bring forgiveness to the whole world, so we should try to follow the example of Jesus and try to forgive others. This is reflected in the Lord's Prayer that Jesus taught: 'forgive us our sins, as we forgive those who sin against us' (Matthew 6:12).

   Islam:
   - Islam teaches that Allah is compassionate and merciful. Surah 64:14 describes Allah forgiving humans for what they have done wrong and suggests this is also how Muslims should act.
   - Muslims believe Islam is a religion of peace and that Allah intends for humanity to live peacefully in the world. To achieve this, Muslims believe they should follow the example of Muhammad, who forgave others and taught about the importance of forgiveness as seen in his final sermon.

112. The death penalty

1. B Capital punishment
2. For example:
   - The death penalty is used to deter other criminals from committing the same crime.
   - The death penalty is used to offer a punishment for the most serious crimes.
   - The death penalty is used to make victims feel safe.
   - The death penalty is used to give justice.
   - The death penalty is used to offer closure to the victim's family.
3. For example:
   Christianity:
   - Some Christians believe the death penalty should not be used as it goes against the sanctity of life. They may argue that all life deserves respect, including the life of a criminal.
   - Some Christians support the use of the death penalty. They may argue that some teachings in the Bible seem to suggest it is acceptable. The Christian Church used the death penalty in the Middle Ages for the most serious crimes, so some Christians may feel it is acceptable for the most serious crimes today, such as murder.

   Islam:
   - Some Muslims believe the death penalty should be used, as certain teachings in the Qur'an suggest it is the appropriate punishment for the most serious crimes, such as murder or adultery. Shari'ah law also supports use of the death penalty.
   - Although the Qur'an teaches that the death penalty is one form of punishment that can be used for serious crimes, it does not say it is the only form of punishment. Some Muslims do not support the death penalty as it goes against the teaching of the sanctity of life and there are other suitable punishments such as life imprisonment.

113. The death penalty

1* Arguments in support:
   - Both the Qur'an and Hadith offer support for the death penalty for the most serious crimes. For example, Hadith Sahih Muslim 16:4152 suggests the death penalty can be given for the crimes of murder, rape, homosexual acts and apostasy (denying the existence of Allah).
   - Muhammad made various statements during his life to support the use of the death penalty and sentenced people to death for the crime of murder. As many Muslims believe they should follow Muhammad's example, some would argue that this means use of the death penalty for serious crimes makes sense.
   - Shari'ah law, the Islamic code of behaviour applied in many Islamic countries, is based on the Qur'an. It states that the death penalty should be used for serious crimes. Indeed, in some Islamic countries such as Afghanistan, Iran and Pakistan, the death penalty is used today.
   - Some Christians may agree with the statement because the Bible teaches that the death penalty can be used for serious crimes. They may look to teachings such as 'Whoever sheds human blood, by humans shall their blood be shed' (Genesis 9:6) and 'with the measure you use, it will be measured to you' (Matthew 7:2) to argue that the death penalty is acceptable.
   - Some Christians may agree with the statement because the Christian Church used the death penalty in the Middle Ages for serious crimes. They may believe there is still a need for the death penalty in today's society.
   - Some non-religious believers may support the use of the death penalty for the most serious crimes as it protects society from dangerous criminals such as murderers. They may also argue that the financial costs of rehabilitating the most dangerous criminals are high and that using the death penalty for murderers would help victims' families feel that justice had been served.

   Arguments in support of other views:
   - Some Muslims may disagree with the death penalty completely, arguing that the Qur'an states that the death penalty is only one punishment option – an alternative is life imprisonment.
   - Muslims believe in the sanctity of life: life is sacred as Allah created it. They may argue that the death penalty conflicts with this teaching.
   - Many Christians may argue that the overall message from Christianity is one of love and forgiveness, which seems to go against the use of the death penalty. For example, Jesus taught that violence is wrong and to 'turn the other cheek'. They may also point to the fact that life is special, as God created it, so should not be ended.
   - Many non-religious believers may oppose the use of the death penalty as the criminal can be seen to escape punishment rather than face justice for their crime through life imprisonment. Also, there is the possibility of an innocent person being executed in error, which cannot be reversed.

114. Religion, crime and punishment: Contrasting beliefs

1. For example:
   Christianity:
   - Many Christians believe the use of corporal punishment goes against the teaching of the sanctity of human life. Life made by God should be respected, not hurt.
   - Christianity teaches that corporal punishment does not support human rights. One of the aims of punishment is to reform criminals, which can be achieved by imprisonment (taking the criminal's freedom away) rather than physical punishment.

   Islam:
   - Islam teaches that a criminal should be given the chance to reform, which can be achieved by imprisonment rather than corporal punishment. Muslims believe Allah created all life, so it is sacred and should be respected at all times.
   - Islam is a religion of peace so corporal punishment goes against this. Muslims believe they should respect life and try to live peacefully with one another, even those who commit crimes.

2. For example:
   Christianity:
   - Christianity teaches that, through prayer, God gives them the strength to forgive others, even when it is difficult to do so. Through the Lord's Prayer, Christians are taught they should always try to forgive others, as they would like God to forgive them. Christians believe they should follow the example of Jesus, who came to Earth to bring forgiveness and reconciliation between God and

173

humanity. Even when dying on the cross, he was able to forgive those who had crucified him.

Islam:
- Islam teaches that there may be some crimes that cannot be forgiven. For these crimes, such as murder and adultery, the death penalty should be used. In these cases, it may be preferable to punish the criminals rather than forgive them.

115. Religion, crime and punishment: Contrasting beliefs

1 For example:
Christianity:
- Christians believe in the sanctity of life and so would not support the use of the death penalty as it means taking life and going against this teaching.
- Christians follow the Ten Commandments, which are rules from God. One of these says 'You shall not murder' (Exodus 20:13), which suggests that taking life for any reason is wrong and against God. Many Christians use this teaching to argue that the death penalty is wrong.

Islam:
- Some Muslims may argue that life is special as Allah created it for a set purpose, so to take life is always wrong. They may not support the use of the death penalty for this reason.

2 For example:
Christianity:
- Many Christians believe the use of corporal punishment goes against the teaching of the sanctity of human life; all life made by God should be respected, not hurt. Christians may also believe corporal punishment does not support human rights. One of the aims of punishment is to reform criminals. This can be achieved by imprisonment (taking the criminal's freedom away) rather than physical punishment.

Islam:
- Some Muslims support the use of physical punishment as it appears in the Qur'an. For example, Surah 24:2 advises that those who are guilty of adultery should be given a physical punishment of lashings.

Theme F: Religion, human rights and social justice

Human rights

116. Prejudice and discrimination

1 B Poverty
2 For example:
Christianity:
- Many Christians believe discrimination is wrong because God created all humans equally 'in his image' (Genesis 1:26).
- Some Christians believe discrimination is wrong because of Jesus' teachings in the Bible. He gave the golden rule of 'do to others what you would have them do to you' (Matthew 7:12). This means that you should treat people the way you would like to be treated and, just as you would not want to be discriminated against, so you should not discriminate against others.

Islam:
- Islam teaches that discrimination is wrong because Allah created all humans so all people deserve equal treatment and respect. Surah 49:13 talks of the way Allah created all humans from one man and one woman, so that humanity 'might know one another'.
- Muslims believe discrimination is wrong because, in his final sermon before his death, Muhammad stressed the importance of treating everyone equally and not discriminating against anyone.

117. Prejudice and discrimination

1* Arguments in support:
- Some Muslims may agree with the statement as they believe Allah created all humans to be equal, although not the same. Surah 49:13 teaches that prejudice and discrimination are wrong between genders as Allah is responsible for all of creation. Men and women are seen to have different roles in Islam, but Muslims are taught these roles complement each other: men are the providers while women look after the children and home. As a Hadith says, 'men and women are equal as the teeth of a comb'.
- Islam teaches that Allah will judge all men and women equally after death for their actions in life. This suggests that men and women should be treated equally in life.
- The Bible teaches that all humans were 'made in the image of God' so most Christians believe men and women deserve equal treatment.
- Jesus did not discriminate between men and women but treated women equally, and with compassion, including the woman being stoned for adultery and the woman who touched his cloak. Christians believe they should follow his example.
- Some non-religious believers may agree with the statement because they believe all humans are equal, although not for any religious reasons. They may say that all people are equal by law and deserve the same human rights.

Arguments in support of other views:
- Some Christians may disagree with the statement because in some Christian denominations, such as Catholicism, women are not allowed to hold positions of authority (for example, priests, cardinals, the pope). These roles are seen to be representing Jesus, who was male.
- Some Muslims may believe only men can hold positions of responsibility within Islam. For example the imam, who leads prayers, is always male.
- Some actions supported by some Muslims suggest that men and women should not be treated the same and suggest ideas of inequality. Ideas may include women being chaperoned by their husbands, women not being allowed to drive or mix freely with men who are not direct family members. There are also supported teachings such as men being allowed to have up to four wives, whereas Muslim women are only allowed one husband.

118. Equality and freedom of religious belief

1 For example:
- Christians/Muslims support human rights because they believe all life is sacred as God/Allah created it, therefore all humans deserve to be treated with respect through the recognition of human rights.
- Christians support human rights because of teachings such as 'treat others as you would like to be treated'.
- Holy books teach about the importance of human life.
- It is a duty of religious believers to stand up for others.
- Human rights are important to achieve fairness and justice in the world.

2 For example:
Christianity:
- Christianity teaches that God made all humans to be equal as they were all made 'in the image of God' (Genesis 1:26).
- Many people at the time of Jesus were considered 'outcasts' and isolated in society, such as the poor, lepers and Gentiles, but Jesus treated them the same, and most Christians believe they should follow Jesus' example. This is also supported by the teaching of Galatian 3:28 ('for you are all one in Christ Jesus').

Islam:
- Islam teaches that all Muslims are part of the ummah and deserve equal treatment. This means that all Muslims, regardless of colour and nationality, should be treated the same, as shown by Surah 30:22: 'the diversity of your languages and your colours'.
- Islam has many practices that demonstrate equality between all humans. Muslims pray at the same time, facing the same way, standing shoulder to shoulder to show equality. This reflects teachings from the last sermon of Muhammad, where he emphasised that all humans are equal.

119. Equality and freedom of religious belief

1. B Equality
2. For example:
   Christianity:
   - Christianity teaches that everyone should have freedom of religion and belief as this is a basic human right. Christians follow teachings such as those from Jesus, who said 'treat others as you would like to be treated', meaning that people should not be treated differently for any reason, including religion and belief.

   Islam:
   - Many Muslims believe everyone should have freedom of religion and belief as they believe Allah will recognise those who are good even if they are not actually Muslim. Some Muslims argue that it does not matter which religion a person belongs to as we are all equal in front of Allah.

120. Social justice

1. D Social justice
2. For example:
   - Many religious believers feel they have a duty from God/Allah to work for social justice.
   - The Bible/Qur'an teaches that social justice is important.
   - Jesus/Muhammad lived by the principles of social justice and religious believers aim to follow their example.
   - Religious practices promote ideas of social justice.
3. For example:
   - Christians/Muslims can provide basic food supplies to those who are living in poverty, such as by donating to a food bank.
   - Christians/Muslims can promote ideas of social justice in their local communities to encourage others to help through community projects.
   - Christians/Muslims can educate others about social justice issues and what they can do to help.
   - Christians/Muslims can volunteer or work for charities.
   - Muslims give Zakah – 2.5 per cent of their annual wealth – to help others.

121. Social justice

1. For example:
   - Muslims/Christians feel social justice is important as Allah/God gave them the duty of helping others.
   - Allah/God will judge people after death on whether they have helped others.
   - Religious texts such as the Qur'an/Bible promote ideas of social justice.
   - Holy books teach that all people are equal and about the importance of reducing inequality in the world.
2*. Arguments in support:
   - Some Christians may agree with the statement as wealth and money are not distributed equally around the world. Smaller numbers of people hold large amounts of wealth, which leaves many people living in poverty. They may argue that God made the world this way and if people are born into and living in poverty, this is God's intention for them. Many influential people (for example, the disciples) achieved many things while they lived in poverty. Although religion can support those living in poverty, it cannot necessarily help everyone and it cannot make all aspects of wealth and money fair.
   - In Mark 10:25, Jesus says the poor will inherit the Kingdom of God ('it is harder for a wealthy man to pass through the eye of a needle than to enter God's Kingdom'). Christians may use this teaching to suggest that there is inequality in the world because some people need to learn to be less greedy and use their wealth to help others.
   - Some Muslims may agree with the statement as, although they work to help reduce the effects of poverty in the world, they cannot make the wealthy give their money away or the poor more wealthy. They would argue that sometimes it is about helping who you can. They may also suggest that if Allah created a world with inequality, this is done for a deliberate purpose and that even though we do not know what this purpose is, we should accept it and work to live up to the standards set by Allah.
   - Some non-religious believers may agree with the statement, arguing that you can help those living in poverty but it is difficult to make the world entirely equal.

   Arguments in support of other views:
   - Many Christians would argue that it is their duty from God to work to support those in society who are living in poverty. The Bible teaches that Christians have a duty to work for social justice. Many churches try to address poverty, for example through the provision of food banks, and many Christian charities such as Christian Aid promote social justice. Many Christians might argue that to accept inequality in the world would be to do nothing about it and this is not what God wants. Jesus taught the importance of helping those in need.
   - The Qur'an teaches Muslims they should work for social justice. One of the Five Pillars of Islam is Zakah, which is an annual charity given by all Muslims to help make the world a fairer place. Muslims believe they have a duty from Allah to support all those who are struggling in the world and to work for social justice. Surah 2:177 says Muslims should 'give wealth, in spite of love for it, to relatives, orphans, the needy, the traveller, those who ask [for help] and for freeing slaves'.
   - Many non-religious believers would disagree with the statement, arguing that to accept inequality in the world is the same as doing nothing about it. They may support fundraising work of local communities to help make the world a fairer place by helping those in need.

Wealth and poverty

122. Responsibilities of wealth

1. For example:
   Christianity:
   - Christians believe they should follow the example of Jesus in caring for others and helping the poor. They can do this by donating money or by volunteering/working for a charity such as Christian Aid.
   - Jesus' teachings in the Bible include the Parable of the Good Samaritan, which shows Christians have a duty to help others in need and to 'treat others as you would like to be treated'.

   Islam:
   - Muslims believe they have duties given to them by Allah, including the Pillar of Zakah, which requires Muslims to give 2.5 per cent of their annual earnings to help the poor.
   - Islam teaches that Allah gave all humans the duty of caring for others. As all Muslims are part of the ummah, they are expected to help the poor where they can.

123. Responsibilities of wealth

1*. Arguments in support:
   - Many Christians would think there are many things they can do to promote social justice and help alleviate poverty in the world, such as providing food banks and volunteering for charity organisations. The Bible teaches that Christians have a duty from God to help others. Teachings from Jesus such as the Parable of the Good Samaritan and 'treat others as you would like to be treated' demonstrate that Christians should always act to help those in poverty.
   - Most Muslims would agree with the statement because they are taught they have a duty from Allah to help others. Therefore, individuals do make a difference to overcoming poverty and it would be wrong not to try to help. Muslims are also encouraged to have the right attitude to wealth by accepting it does not belong to them but to Allah. They are encouraged to share what they have with others as a duty through Zakah. There are many Islamic charities, including Islamic Relief and Muslim Aid, that work all over the world to tackle poverty.

   Arguments in support of other views:
   - Some religious believers, including Christians and Muslims, may disagree with the statement, because

individuals can make some difference by helping the poor, but they may feel that the work of individuals is not enough to have a major impact. They may argue that individuals need to take responsibility for their own lives and it takes major organisations or governments to make a real difference in tackling the worldwide problems associated with poverty.
- Some non-religious believers may argue that governments often cause poverty by allowing the exploitation of individuals and therefore responsibility should be given to them to overcome poverty in the world. They may argue that we should try to help others, as all life is valuable, yet it is not our duty to do so and they will not feel there are religious reasons to do so either.

124. Exploitation of the poor

1* Arguments in support:
- Christianity teaches that money is a gift from God and should be earned honestly and treated respectfully. Most Christians believe it is wrong to abuse people by lending money with excessive interest charges. Some Bible teachings support this view, including 'Love your neighbour as yourself' (Mark 12:31) and teachings on God creating all humans to be equal.
- Lending money in Islam is forbidden if the lender benefits from interest. Surah 30:39 talks of not finding favour with Allah through excessive lending for profit. Muslims are encouraged to share their money and help others rather than exploit them. There are Muslim banks that lend money without making interest on it.
- Some non-religious believers may argue that inequality in the world is fuelled by lending money for profit. When financial institutions loan money, wealthy people tend to be given lower interest rates, whereas poorer people, who are most in need of financial help, have to pay higher rates. This makes poverty and inequality even worse.

Arguments in support of other views:
- Many people, both religious and non-religious, may argue that lending money for profit is not wrong as businesses need to make profits in order to survive in the modern world, as long as any profit is not excessive and does not exploit others. Some Christians and Muslims may suggest that traditional Bible or Qur'anic teachings need to be updated in line with modern life as some teachings may be considered out of date for the economic and financial realities of our technological, modern-day world.

125. Exploitation of the poor

1 For example:
- The poor may be paid unfairly for the work they complete.
- The poor may be treated unequally compared to others.
- The poor may be required to pay excessive interest on loans.
- The poor are at risk of human trafficking.
- The poor are made to endure poor working conditions.

2 For example:
Christianity:
- Christians do not accept human trafficking under any circumstance as they believe all human life is sacred and 'made in the image of God' (Genesis 1:26).
- Key teachings in Christianity include agape love which is unconditional love for everyone as taught through Jesus in the Bible. As human trafficking shows no respect for human life, Christians believe they have a duty to help those in this position who are being exploited.

Islam:
- Many Muslims believe human trafficking is wrong because they accept the sanctity of life argument, which teaches that all human life is sacred as Allah created it, as described in Surah 49:13. Therefore it is wrong to traffic people, as this disrespects their humanity and allows others to profit from this cruelty.
- Many Muslims believe human trafficking is wrong as Allah gave all humans the duty to care for and not harm each other, as taught in the Qur'an. This would include standing up against those who are exploiting vulnerable people in society through human trafficking.

126. Poverty and charity

1 A Poverty
2 For example:
Christian Aid; CAFOD; Tearfund; Muslim Aid; Islamic Relief.
3 For example:
Christianity:
- Christians believe it is important to show compassion towards others. Ephesians 4:32 teaches 'Be kind and compassionate to one another' and Jesus taught 'love your neighbour'. Christians believe they can do this by giving money to charity in order to help others.
- Christians believe helping the poor through charity will bring favour with God. They accept that humans were given the responsibility of caring for God's creation, which includes humans. Proverbs 14:31 says 'whoever is kind to the needy honours God'.

Islam:
- Muslims are taught about the importance of charity through the third Pillar of Islam, Zakah. They give 2.5 per cent of their annual earnings to charity to help those living in poverty. Surah 2:177 describes the importance of giving Zakah.
- Muslims are encouraged to perform sadaqah, which is any good deed done for others. This could involve giving a donation to charity or giving time to help another person. Muslims believe they have a duty to care for others and show compassion, as seen in Surah 2:110.

127. Poverty and charity

1 For example:
- People in poverty can help themselves by actively looking for a job.
- People in poverty can help themselves by accepting help but not relying on it.
- People in poverty can help themselves by budgeting carefully.
- People in poverty can help themselves by using their talents in a positive way.
- People in poverty can help themselves by actively looking for solutions to their problems.
- People in poverty can help themselves by praying to God/Allah.

2 For example:
Christianity:
- Christians look to teachings in the Bible such as the Parable of the Talents to explain why they should help those in poverty. The parable teaches that we should help others to become self-sufficient rather than just giving them charity, as this will mean more to them in the long term.
- Christians believe Jesus gave the commandment to 'love thy neighbour' (Mark 12:31), which means they should help others, including those in poverty. Christians believe they should follow Jesus' example by helping those living in poverty.

Islam:
- Islam teaches Muslims the importance of helping others through the third Pillar of Islam, Zakah. Muslims annually give 2.5 per cent of their earnings to support those in poverty as they believe it is a duty given to them by Allah. This can be seen in Surah 2:177, which describes the righteous as those who give their wealth to others.
- Muslims believe Allah will reward them in the afterlife for the way they have helped others. Muhammad taught in a Hadith that helping those in poverty would get the generous man to paradise. Muslims try to follow the teachings of Muhammad and his example.

128. Religion, human rights and social justice: Contrasting beliefs

1 For example:
Christianity:
- Christians believe all humans – both men and women – are equal as God made all humanity. The Bible teaches that God made all humans 'in the image of God' (Genesis 1:26). This suggests women in religion should have the same rights as men.

- Christians follow the example of Jesus who did not discriminate between men and women but treated them the same. This is shown today in the Protestant Church, which allows female bishops, in this way supporting equality in status between men and women.

Islam:
- Islam teaches that, as Allah made all humans, they are equal. Muhammad also taught that it was important to treat everyone the same, which suggests the need for equality in status for women and men in Islam.

2 For example:
Christianity:
- Christians believe they should use their wealth to help others as this is a key teaching from Jesus. Many Christians choose to tithe, which is giving 10 per cent of their earnings to the Church to help those who are poor and needy.
- Christians believe they should use their wealth unselfishly to help others. This could involve giving money to charities such as Christian Aid or CAFOD, which use the money to help reduce poverty in the world.

Islam:
- Muslims believe they should use their wealth to help others. They can do this through Zakah, which is the third Pillar of Islam and is the duty to give 2.5 per cent of their earnings to charity to help the poor.
- Muslims are told to use their money wisely and honestly, avoiding gambling and lending money for profit as this takes advantage of people.

129. Religion, human rights and social justice: Contrasting beliefs

1 For example:
Christianity:
- Christians believe wealth should be used in unselfish ways to help others. They can choose to support charities such as Christian Aid, which use wealth from charitable donations to tackle poverty. They may see it as their duty from God to share their wealth.
- Some Christians believe wealth is a gift from God, therefore it is not a sin to be wealthy and nor is it a sin to make profit, although exploiting others for money is wrong. They might argue that being wealthy means they can contribute to a healthy economy and they can afford to help others.

Islam:
- Islam teaches that Muslims have a duty to share their wealth with others as Allah created all people to be equal, with all members of the ummah seen as equally important. Muslims have a duty through completing one of the Five Pillars of Islam, Zakah, to give 2.5 per cent of their annual wealth to share with others.
- Muslims are taught that it is wrong to use their money for profit and they should avoid gambling. Muslims have access to special Islamic banks that lend money, such as mortgages, without making a profit.

2 For example:
Christianity:
- Most Christians believe both men and women are equal as the Bible teaches that God made all humans 'in the image of God' (Genesis 1:26). Therefore, many believe both women and men can hold positions of authority in the Church. This can be seen in the Protestant Church, which allows women to hold the position of bishop.
- Some Christians believe only men can hold positions of authority within the Church. Although they recognise that God made men and women to be equal, in the Catholic Church men hold all Church positions as this is seen to represent Jesus, who was male.

Islam:
- Islam teaches that men and women are equal but were not made the same by Allah. Men and women are seen to have different roles within the faith. Only men are given positions of authority within Islam as women are not allowed to hold such roles.

Theme G: St Mark's Gospel I

130. John's preparation for Jesus' ministry

1 A Ministry
2 For example:
- John is important to Christians today as St Mark's Gospel explains that he prepared the way for Jesus as the Messiah. Mark 1:1–8 describes how John introduced ideas to people that would later be taught by Jesus, which helped Jesus and his teachings to be accepted.
- In Mark 1:1–8, John baptises people with the Holy Spirit in the River Jordan. He is important as he reflects key Christian ideas about repentance and the forgiveness of sins, which is also the message of Jesus and Christianity.

131. Jesus' baptism and temptation

1 For example:
- John baptised Jesus.
- Heaven was 'torn open'.
- A dove flew down.
- God spoke, saying 'You are my Son, who I love; with you I am well pleased.'

2* Arguments in support:
- Jesus' baptism can be understood to have more importance as it shows the truth of the prophecy of Jesus being the Messiah. During Jesus' baptism, he is publicly recognised by John as the Son of God and the one that the people are waiting for. Other signs of Jesus' divine nature include heaven being 'torn open' and the dove descending.
- The concept of baptism is central to the Christian faith as it symbolises entrance into the Christian Church. The fact that baptism continues to be a sacrament and rite of passage for Christians today gives it more relevance and importance than Jesus' temptation.
- The representation of the Father, Son and Holy Spirit are all visible elements within the baptism of Jesus, so some Christians may point to the fact that Jesus' baptism reinforces understanding of the Trinity, which is used by Christians to understand God. This suggests that Jesus' baptism is more important than his temptation.

Arguments in support of other views:
- Some Christians may view the baptism and temptations of Jesus as having equal importance, as one came after the other. After Jesus was baptised in the River Jordan, he went out into the wilderness where he faced the three temptations.
- Some Christians may argue that the temptation of Jesus holds a stronger message for Christians today than his baptism. Christ's temptation indicates that just as Jesus was tempted by the devil, so we, too, have to resist daily temptations in our lives in order to avoid sin and follow the path of God.

132. Miracles of Jesus I

1 C Healing a man with a broken arm
2* Arguments in support:
- For many Christians, the miracles Jesus performed, such as healing the paralysed man, show that he was the Son of God, as normal humans cannot do what Jesus did. Many Christians also believe Jesus' miracles prove he was the Son of God as they demonstrate God's power and loving nature acting through Jesus.
- For many Christians, Jesus' miracles prove that he was the Son of God because they reflect the nature of God as omnipotent and benevolent. This is shown by, for example, Jesus performing miracles such as bringing someone back from the dead.
- That many people witnessed Jesus' miracles and they were recorded in the Bible reinforces the importance of Jesus as the Son of God.
- The ultimate miracle accepted by many Christians is the resurrection, which is central to the Christian religion. For many Christians, Jesus' resurrection provides proof that Jesus was the Son of God because he overcame death.

Arguments in support of other views:
- Some people may argue that, as the Bible was written so long ago and before modern scientific methods, some events that people could

177

not explain may simply have been misinterpreted as 'miracles'. They may argue that there is no proof these miracles took place as described. Therefore, 'miracles' cannot be relied upon to prove that Jesus was the Son of God.
- Some Christians believe the Bible is the word of God but do not place as much importance on miracles. They may argue that Jesus dying on the cross and his actual resurrection is evidence enough that he was the Son of God. They do not need the further existence of miracles he performed during his life to confirm this for them.
- Some Christians may argue that the events surrounding the birth of Jesus, his ability to predict what would happen to him and the transfiguration may be taken as stronger evidence of Jesus being the Son of God than the miracles themselves.

133. Miracles of Jesus II
1 For example:
- For many Christians, miracles prove the existence of God as they believe ordinary people cannot perform miracles.
- For many Christians, miracles show that God cares for his creation.
- For many Christians, miracles show that God wants to be involved in the world.
- For many Christians, miracles provide comfort and hope for Christians.
- For many Christians, miracles help Christians to confirm their faith.
2 For example:
- The feeding of the five thousand is important for Christians today as an example of the power of God through Jesus. Christians understand God to be omnipotent and, in this miracle in St Mark's Gospel, Jesus is seen to have this power as he ensures that every person in the crowd of five thousand is fed from five loaves and two fishes, which would normally be impossible.
- St Mark's Gospel shows through the story of the feeding of the five thousand the importance of having faith in Jesus. It suggests that because people had faith in Jesus as the Son of God, this allowed the miracle to occur and strengthened Christian understanding of the power of faith.
- The miracle of the feeding of the five thousand proves to Christians today that God cares for his creation. St Mark's Gospel states that he sent Jesus, his only Son, to Earth to atone for humanity's sins. Through the use of miracles such as the feeding of the five thousand, Jesus was able to prove that he was indeed the Son of God. Jesus also set a loving example for all Christians today, which is important in showing them that the way to God is by loving others.

134. Caesarea Philippi and the transfiguration
1 For example:
- Christians believe the conversation at Caesarea Philippi was the first time the disciples accepted Jesus as the Messiah.
- It is seen as a turning point in the ministry of Jesus. After the event, the ministry of Jesus became more private.
- The prediction of Jesus dying on the cross and being resurrected is part of the conversation.
- Jesus warned his disciples not to tell other people that he was the Messiah.
2 For example:
- Some Christians view the transfiguration as a unique miracle, yet Jesus did not perform it. At the transfiguration, Peter, James and John see the prophets Elijah and Moses with Jesus. As Elijah and Moses were dead, this shows how the laws of nature were broken by this miracle.
- Some Christians believe the transfiguration shows Jesus being recognised as the Son of God. During the transfiguration, God speaks to Peter, James and John and declares Jesus to be his Son and that they should listen to him.
- Some Christians believe the transfiguration proves that there is eternal life with God in heaven as Moses and Elijah, who died many years before, appeared. For many Christians, this demonstrates there is an afterlife that humans can share if they follow Jesus' example.

135. Passion prediction and James and John's request
1* Arguments in support:
- Jesus sharing the news of his death through the passion prediction would allow the disciples time to come to terms with the fact that he was going to die. He felt that understanding why he had to die as part of the prophecy would enable the disciples to accept his death more readily as having a higher purpose, which would support them in being able to continue his work in the world after his death.
- Jesus was sacrificed so that God would forgive the sins of humanity and, through Jesus sharing this prediction with the disciples, it helped them to understand the way he approached his death and his sacrifice.
- Through Jesus sharing the prediction of his death and resurrection and the events he described coming true, he was proving that he was the Son of God to his disciples as no normal person would be able to predict what was going to happen so accurately nor rise again from the dead.

Arguments in support of other views:
- Some people might argue that Jesus telling the disciples the prophecy of his death scared them and caused them to lose faith. They may have felt that it meant being a follower of Jesus was too dangerous and that if Jesus faced the punishment he predicted, they did not want to be part of it. It could be seen that, when Peter betrayed Jesus by denying him three times, this was due to fear as a result of the prophecy.
- Some people may argue that it was not necessary for Jesus to share the events of the Passion with the disciples as not doing so would not have changed the events happening. It could be argued that the disciples would have recognised Jesus as the Son of God from the event of his resurrection, without the prophecy.
- Many Christians may argue that Jesus taught by example and his key messages were those of unconditional love and the power of forgiveness. The disciples were able to learn these messages from Jesus without knowing the prophecy of his death and resurrection. It is even possible to suggest that knowing and worrying about these events may have prevented them from fully engaging with the teachings Jesus shared with them.

136. The story of Bartimaeus
1 For example:
- In the story of Bartimaeus in St Mark's Gospel, Jesus is known as the Son of David as he was born in Bethlehem, which is known as the City of David. As God had promised David that his throne would be established for ever, many Christians view Jesus as the rightful King of the Jews.
- Jesus is also referred to in the story of Bartimaeus as a rabbi. This means 'teacher' and refers to the idea that Jesus is seen to have authority through his teachings.
- Jesus is also referred to in the story of Bartimaeus as Jesus of Nazareth, as Nazareth is the place where he grew up and where he began his ministry.
2 For example:
- The story of Bartimaeus includes a number of names that Jesus is given, such as Jesus of Nazareth, Son of David and Rabbi. These show the many roles Jesus had and the different ways in which he was known and understood, with each of the names meaning something different (for example, 'rabbi' means teacher). This helps to give Christians today a better understanding of who Jesus was and, through him, a closer connection to God.
- The story of Bartimaeus is important for Christians today as it shows the importance of faith. It was only because Bartimaeus had complete faith in Jesus being the Son of God that he refused to let him pass, and this meant Jesus stopped and restored his sight.

- The story of Bartimaeus is a healing miracle that Jesus performed. This is important for Christians today as it reinforces belief in Jesus' divine power as the Son of God. Through the Bible account of many people witnessing Jesus stopping to heal Bartimaeus, Christians today can better understand God's characteristics (such as his omnipotence and omnibenevolence).

137. The entry into Jerusalem
1. D On the back of a donkey, happy and pleased to see people
2. For example:
   - Jesus entered Jerusalem on a donkey. This is important for Christians today as it shows his humility and lack of self-importance. Although Jesus was divine, representing God on Earth, he was also human and willing to ride a donkey, which at the time was not the kind of animal that important people rode.
   - Jesus was happy and cheerful as he entered Jerusalem. This is important for Christians today as it shows that, although his death was sad, it would fulfil the prophecy of Jesus saving humanity from sin. Jesus' entry into Jerusalem suggests how Christians today can feel joyful about his sacrifice and the presence of God in their lives.
   - Jesus entered Jerusalem in front of witnesses and was not hiding from people or trying to escape what he knew would happen (his crucifixion). This is important for Christians today as it gives Christians the strength to face the things they find difficult and to realise the importance of following him in order to find God.

138. The Last Supper
1. B One of the disciples would betray him
2. For example:
   - Christians believe Jesus gave instructions at the Last Supper for how he should be remembered, which are part of the Eucharist service.
   - The Last Supper marks the beginning of the events of the crucifixion and resurrection, which are central in Christianity.
   - The Last Supper allows Christians to remember Jesus' sacrifice.
   - The Last Supper is where the symbols of the bread and wine come from.
   - The Last Supper represents a key sacrament celebrated by Christians today.
3. For example:
   - Jesus took bread and gave thanks for it.
   - Jesus told the disciples that the bread represented his body.
   - Jesus told the disciples that the wine represented his blood.
   - The disciples were given the instruction to re-enact the Last Supper in remembrance of him.
   - Jesus shared the meal with his disciples.

139. Jesus in Gethsemane and the trial
1. For example:
   - Christians believe the trial was illegal as people gave false testimony against Jesus.
   - Christians believe Jesus was accused of blasphemy.
   - Christians believe Jesus was asked if he was the Messiah.
   - Christians believe the elders decided Jesus should be put to death.
2. For example:
   - The arrest and trials of Jesus are important to Christians because they reflect the unfair way in which Jesus was treated and the injustice of this. For example, Jesus' trial in front of the Jewish elders was an illegal trial. St Mark's Gospel describes how people were brought into court to lie about Jesus and that, based on these lies, the authorities decided that Jesus was guilty of blasphemy.
   - The arrest of Jesus in the Garden of Gethsemane, as explained in Mark 14:32–52, shows how Jesus accepted what was about to happen to him, even though he knew he was not guilty. When his disciples tried to use violence to prevent him from being arrested, Jesus told them to respond peacefully. This shows Christians that they should behave peacefully too.
   - The arrest and trials of Jesus are important because they brought true the prophecy that Jesus made at the Last Supper: that he would be arrested after one of the disciples betrayed him. For Christians, this is further evidence of Jesus' spiritual powers and that he was the Son of God.

140. The trial before Pilate, the crucifixion and burial
1* Arguments in support:
   - It was Pilate who chose to give the crowd the final decision on which prisoner should be executed, so he is responsible for the decision to kill Jesus. Pilate appeared to think that Jesus was not guilty so, if he had not given the crowd this choice, it is possible that Jesus would not have been put to death.
   - Pilate had the opportunity to release Jesus when the Jewish authorities first brought him. Jesus was accused of the crime of pretending to be 'King of the Jews' and, when Pilate asked Jesus if this was so, Jesus replied saying 'You have said so' (St Mark's Gospel). If Pilate had been stronger and made the decision that Jesus was innocent of this crime, it could be argued that Jesus would not have been crucified.

   Arguments in support of other views:
   - Some may feel that as Jesus' death was prophesised it was inevitable and so no one is ultimately to blame for his death. God sent Jesus to Earth with the purpose of dying on the cross to atone for the sins of humanity. If this were indeed God's intention, it would not have mattered who did what before Jesus' death as his death was predestined and would always have happened in that way.
   - Some may see the elders as more responsible for Jesus' death. They held an illegal trial where Jesus was not given the opportunity to defend himself against the charges. They also took Jesus to Pilate and asked for him to be sentenced.
   - Some blame Jesus' death on Judas, one of Jesus' disciples, who betrayed Jesus by leading the guards to where he was in the Garden of Gethsemane and identifying him. This ultimately led to Jesus being arrested and crucified.

141. The empty tomb
1. For example:
   - Some Christians see Jesus' resurrection as evidence of a miracle that shows God's power and nature. For many Christians, having faith in Jesus and accepting the power of God means recognising that sometimes events are miracles that cannot be explained scientifically.
   - Many Christians today accept modern science alongside ideas of religion and some believe some aspects of the resurrection may be symbolic.
   - Some Christians may look to differing accounts of the resurrection in order to understand this event. The four Gospels all give different accounts of what happened so some Christians may choose to follow and understand just one Gospel whereas others may look to all of the accounts to provide a complete answer.
2* Arguments in support:
   - The resurrection can be seen as the ultimate miracle as only God has the power to bring someone who has died back to life.
   - The resurrection was prophesised by Jesus and happened exactly as he said. Many Christians believe this shows how close Jesus was to God and helps emphasise that the resurrection proves God exists.
   - Many Christians may argue that the resurrection is more than enough evidence to prove that he was special and was the Son of God and so must be proof of God.

   Arguments in support of other views:
   - Some Christians may argue that, as the Bible was written so long ago, it needs reinterpreting to reflect modern scientific knowledge. They may feel that the resurrection cannot provide convincing evidence of God's existence.
   - Some Christians may argue that, although Jesus' resurrection provides good evidence that God exists,

other sources of evidence of God's existence, such as personal religious experiences, provide more personal and definitive proof of his existence.
- Non-religious believers do not believe in God and do not see the Bible as a factual account of what happened. They may argue that modern science proves that resurrection is impossible.

Theme H: St Mark's Gospel II

142. The Kingdom of God I

1   C House of God
2   For example:
- Beliefs about the Kingdom of God help Christians to understand heaven. Jesus taught that when the final judgement comes after death, all those who accept God as king will be in the Kingdom of God. Those who have not accepted him with be outside of it. St Mark's Gospel tells us that Jesus taught at the Last Supper that people would meet him again and share wine with him in the Kingdom of God.
- Beliefs about the Kingdom of God help Christians to live in the way they believe God intends. They believe this will help them achieve a place in the Kingdom of God after death. Jesus taught 'Love your neighbour as yourself... There is no commandment greater' (Mark 12:29–31), and Christians understand that putting this teaching into action will mean they can get closer to God and be rewarded with eternal life.
- Beliefs about the Kingdom of God help Christians to be united as a Christian community. Christians celebrate this through the Eucharist, when they share in the wine that Jesus speaks about in Mark 14:24, when he says that the next time he shares this with others will be in the Kingdom of God.

143. The Kingdom of God II

1   For example:
- The Parable of the Sower.
- The Parable of the Growing Seed.
- The Parable of the Mustard Seed.
- Jesus and the children.
- Jesus and the rich man.
2* Arguments in support:
- Some Christians may argue that the teachings from Jesus on the Kingdom of God are less relevant today because they are unclear and at times contradictory. This may lead them to dismiss Jesus' teachings on the Kingdom of God in favour of some of his other teachings (for example, those about helping others or agape love). They may feel these teachings are clearer and therefore more relevant.
- Some non-religious believers may argue that scientific views today contradict anything offered by religion and that there is no physical proof of God's existence in any case, so all religious teachings are irrelevant.
- Some people may claim that society today is very different to how it was in the time of Jesus. Therefore, many of Jesus' teachings about the Kingdom of God are irrelevant because the issues facing people today are different. For example, people may be more focused on making the most of the life they are living now rather than placing much consideration on how to access the Kingdom of God in the afterlife.

Arguments in support of other views:
- Most Christians would argue that all Jesus' teachings are relevant today, especially those concerning beliefs about the Kingdom of God. Jesus used parables to help people understand how to enter heaven, which is a fundamental aim for every Christian.
- Many Christians would argue that Jesus' parables (such as the Parable of the Sower, the Parable of the Growing Seed and the Parable of the Mustard Seed) have important messages (for example, what the Kingdom of God is thought to be like, how to achieve entry into the Kingdom of God, the importance of living life correctly to get closer to God) that never lose relevance. These messages help Christians today understand how God wants them to live.
- Some of the parables Jesus taught about the Kingdom of God may be considered too difficult to help some people understand his teachings. Some Christians may need them to be explained or interpreted first so they may argue that, although relevant, they are challenging.

144. Jesus' relationships: Women

1   B Jesus accepted women into his inner circle of trusted people
2   For example:
- The way Jesus treated women is important for Christians today as it suggests how Christians should treat women. Jesus' example reflects his ideas about equality between men and women. Although Jesus' treatment of women was considered radical at the time, it is in line with current equality laws in Britain. Reference could be made to the anointing at Bethany in Mark 14:1–9, when Jesus defended the actions of a woman.
- The way Jesus treated women gave them more status and authority. This is seen today within the Church of England, where women can now hold positions of authority such as bishop. Jesus showed that men and women are equal before God and so can also both be rewarded by God. In the account of the widow at the treasury (Mark 12:41–44), a widow gives only a small amount of money compared to the amount men were able to give, yet it is seen as meaningful to God.
- The way that Jesus treated women suggests that it is wrong to discriminate today. In the anointing at Bethany (Mark 14:1–9) or the widow at the treasury (Mark 12:41–44), Jesus spoke positively about women's contributions. This reinforces other Christian teachings that suggest men and women should be treated equally.

145. Jesus' relationships: Gentiles and tax collectors

1   For example:
- Jesus showed that it is wrong to discriminate against someone just because of who they are.
- Jesus put teachings of equality into action.
- Jesus demonstrated the teaching of 'love one another'.
- Jesus set the standard for how people should be treated in society.
- Jesus challenged prejudice towards, and negative stereotypes of, some groups in society. This is important to Christians today as it reminds them of the importance of equality.
2   For example:
- Jesus' treatment of Gentiles and tax collectors is shown to be important as it went against the prejudicial way in which they were usually treated at the time. Jesus did not discriminate against any group in society, as shown in Mark 7:25–26 when a non-Jewish woman begs for his help in healing her daughter. Jesus' actions show that his healing power is for everyone.
- Jesus showed through eating with Levi, a tax collector, someone whom many people assumed he would not associate with (Mark 2:16–17), that he challenged traditional stereotypes and that it is important to care for all God's people with love.
- By healing the child of a Gentile, as seen in Mark 7:25–26, Jesus showed people how to behave and did not discriminate between those who were Jewish and those who were not. He taught that God's love was for everyone.

146. Jesus' relationships: The sick

1   For example:
- The story of the man with leprosy.
- The story of the demon-possessed boy.
- The story of the widow at the treasury.
- The story of the anointing at Bethany.
- The story of the Greek woman's daughter.
2   For example:
- Many Christians today believe the healing parables told by Jesus show the importance of people having faith. For example, in the story of the demon-possessed boy (Mark 9:14–29), the father needed to have faith in order that the demon could be removed and his son healed.

- Many Christians believe Jesus' healing parables show what God is like. This can be seen through the healing of the man with leprosy (Mark 1:40–45), when Jesus cures a man who was isolated in society because of his condition. The omnibenevolence and power of God is shown through Jesus' healing powers and actions.
- Christians believe Jesus' healing parables are important as they reinforce many teachings in the Bible, such as those on the way people should be treated or beliefs about equality. For example, the accounts of the man being cured of leprosy or the healing of the epileptic boy reinforce other Christian teachings such as 'treat others as you would like to be treated' or 'love your neighbour'.

147. Faith and discipleship I

1 For example:
- Some fundamental Christians believe the disciples were actually able to speak different languages, drive out demons and drink poison, as described in Mark 16. They may have a literal interpretation of the passage, believing that the disciples were actually given special physical powers in order to carry out the mission Jesus had given them.
- Other Christians believe the instructions that Jesus gave to the disciples are symbolic of the mission given to all Christians in their duty to share the Christian faith with others. They do not take the account literally as saying the apostles could drive out demons, drink poison and speak in tongues, instead understanding this as a metaphorical description of the spiritual strength they had to deal with the difficult situations they encountered.

2* Arguments in support:
- Jesus' disciples risked their lives to follow him. The Romans put Jesus to death for preaching and teaching God's message so those following Jesus would have risked similar treatment. The example of Peter denying Jesus suggests how afraid Peter was of being punished for following Jesus.
- Jesus was able to use the power of God to show people the way of following him. For example, performing miracles was one way of people accepting who he was. The disciples faced this added challenge in being seen as important. Although Mark 16:14–20 suggests the disciples had the power to continue Jesus' mission after his death, many do not interpret this literally and know the dangers (including persecution, threats and mocking) the disciples would have faced in sharing their faith with others.
- The disciples had to endure hardships and suffering. This included having to make the sacrifice of giving up their belongings, say goodbye to their families and potentially face daily acts of suffering by not having sufficient food and being persecuted by others.

Arguments in support of other views:
- Some Christians may disagree with the statement, pointing out that the disciples were given the tools they needed in order to perform the role they had been chosen for. They might argue that Jesus had chosen the disciples specifically and had prepared them well for what would happen after his death.
- Although the role of a disciple was dangerous, it was also incredibly rewarding. The ultimate reward of eternal life gave the disciples the strength to carry out the mission they had been given. They may argue that rather than being an 'impossible role', being a disciple was a very privileged position and a unique role.
- Some Christians may argue that the disciples were under the protection of Jesus and therefore God, so they did not need to worry about the hardships or violence they encountered. The role of a disciple meant putting trust in God and accepting his love and the fact that he would not abandon them.

148. Faith and discipleship II

1 D The disciple Peter would deny knowing Jesus
2 For example:
- Many Christians see the role of Jesus' disciples as a privileged one of great spiritual reward, despite the challenges they faced at the time. For example, Jesus told the disciples that, although they could face persecution as his disciples, ultimately they would be rewarded with eternal life in heaven.
- Other Christians may argue that the role of Jesus' disciples was extremely challenging. For example, they had to give up their normal lives and family in order to follow him. They also faced persecution and ill treatment from others. Many of the disciples suffered in these ways, which can be seen in the example of Peter, who denied knowing Jesus as he was afraid of how he might be persecuted too.

Published by Pearson Education Limited, 80 Strand, London, WC2R 0RL.
www.pearsonschoolsandfecolleges.co.uk

Text and illustrations © Pearson Education Ltd 2019
Typeset by Kamae Design
Produced by Newgen Publishing UK
Cover illustration by Eoin Coveney

The right of Tanya Hill to be identified as author of this work has been asserted by her in accordance with the Copyright, Designs and Patents Act 1988.

First published 2019

22 21 20 19
10 9 8 7 6 5 4 3 2 1

British Library Cataloguing in Publication Data
A catalogue record for this book is available from the British Library

ISBN 978 1 292 21101 5

Copyright notice
All rights reserved. No part of this publication may be reproduced in any form or by any means (including photocopying or storing it in any medium by electronic means and whether or not transiently or incidentally to some other use of this publication) without the written permission of the copyright owner, except in accordance with the provisions of the Copyright, Designs and Patents Act 1988 or under the terms of a licence issued by the Copyright Licensing Agency, Barnard's Inn, 86 Fetter Lane, London EC4A 1EN(www.cla.co.uk). Applications for the copyright owner's written permission should be addressed to the publisher.

Printed in Slovakia by Neografia

Acknowledgements
Text Credits:
P 149-152, 155 –156-164, 167-171, 173-174, 176-177, 179-181: Scripture quotations taken from The Holy Bible, New International Version® NIV® Copyright © 1973 1978 1984 2011 by Biblica, Inc. TM, Used by permission. All rights reserved worldwide; **P 152-153, 155, 158-161, 163-164, 167-168, 170-172, 174, 175:** The Qur'ān: With Sūrah Introductions and Appendices, Saheeh International Translation, Edited by A.B. al-Mehri, The Qur'ān Project (www.quranproject.org), ISBN 978-0-9548665-4-9, © 2010 Maktabah Booksellers and Publishers; **P 158:** The English Translation of Sahih Al Bukhari With the Arabic Text, by Muhammad Ibn Ismail Bukhari , Muhammad Muhsin Khan, Al-Saadawi Publication, © 1996 Darussalam; **P 157, 161, 167:** Scripture quotations are from the ESV® Bible (The Holy Bible, English Standard Version®), copyright © 2001 by Crossway, a publishing ministry of Good News Publishers. Used by permission. All rights reserved; **P 167:** Ignatius Bible (RSV)- Revised Standard Version- Catholic Edition Bible, 2nd Edition, ISBN: 9780898708349, © 2005 Ignatius Press; **P 171-172, 174:** The Holy Bible, Berean Study Bible, BSB Copyright ©2016, 2018 by Bible Hub, Used by Permission. All Rights Reserved Worldwide; **P 171, 173:** The Holy Bible, New Living Translation, copyright ©1996, 2004, 2015 by Tyndale House Foundation. Used by permission of Tyndale House Publishers, Inc., Carol Stream, Illinois 60188. All rights reserved;

Note from the publisher
Pearson has robust editorial processes, including answer and fact checks, to ensure the accuracy of the content in this publication, and every effort is made to ensure this publication is free of errors. We are, however, only human, and occasionally errors do occur. Pearson is not liable for any misunderstandings that arise as a result of errors in this publication, but it is our priority to ensure that the content is accurate. If you spot an error, please do contact us at resourcescorrections@pearson.com so we can make sure it is corrected.